Untold
Civil Rights
Stories

ASIAN AMERICANS SPEAK OUT FOR JUSTICE

STEWART KWOH & RUSSELL C. LEONG

EDITORS

To Steve, Makiko, Michael +
Ken,

from Stewart Kwoh

RESOURCES FOR STUDENTS, TEACHERS
AND COMMUNITIES

ASIAN PACIFIC AMERICAN LEGAL CENTER

UCLA ASIAN AMERICAN STUDIES CENTER

Printed in the United States of America.

ISBN: 0-934052-43

Editors: Stewart Kwoh and Russell C. Leong
Multicultural Curriculum Consultant: Esther R. Taira
Project Consultant: Don T. Nakanishi
Book Design: JL Mayor
Proofreading: Stephanie D. Santos, George Johnston
Copyediting (phase one): Malcolm Kao, Ellen Wu

"*Education Through Struggle*" cover mural by Darryl Mar, photographed by Mary Uyematsu Kao

"For those whose stories built our communities, Untold Civil Rights Stories is dedicated — to the women and men who are no longer with us — but whose courage and boldness foretell the future."

— *The Editors*

Untold Civil Rights Stories

Contents

Photo: from left, the Honorable Judy Chu, L.A. Mayor Antonio Villaraigosa, Stewart Kwoh, Ismael Ileto and Robin Toma at the Japanese American National Museum, Los Angeles.

Introduction

Stewart Kwoh

Hidden Stories, Unsung Heroes

As I was growing up, I watched Martin Luther King Jr., Cesar Chavez, and Nelson Mandela fight for social justice by confronting and challenging the inequalities that affected their communities. These courageous public figures of different ethnic and racial backgrounds helped me to recognize the types of injustices happening everyday to those closest to me in my own life and community.

One of my first and most vivid realizations of this occurred when I was a middle school student. My church pastor, who was white, was nearly killed during a peaceful demonstration in Alabama in the 1960s. The demonstration was in response to the brutal murders of four African American girls in a church bombing by white supremacists. It was a result of such experiences that I began to develop a consciousness of how all individuals could be affected by racism and discrimination.

"I have always admired the ability of individuals to speak out, to articulate the connections between communities, and to protest against social injustice with just ideas."
— *Stewart Kwoh*

Photo: Law students Stewart Kwoh (right) and Mike Eng (third from right) assisting people being frisked by police while entering a courthouse in 1974.

There are tremendous leaders in all of our communities. The United States is a nation of diversity and California's population is among the most varied in ethnic, religious, and cultural groups. One of the fascinating and inspiring characteristics of these individuals is that they have done not only extraordinary things for their own communities, but have also built bridges with other racial and ethnic communities. For this reason, I like to call these individuals "boundary crossing leaders," for they embody the true essence of leadership for the 21st century — leaders who can build bridges across racial and other lines.

Nearly all American ethnic groups, particularly people of color, face a similar challenge — either sparse coverage of their community heroes or stereotyped coverage of their communities. We can all gain insights into real U.S. history by learning of the contributions of individual Asian Americans, Pacific Islanders, African Americans, Latinos, American Indians, and others. We can see the many ways lives and experiences parallel and touch each other.

The challenges faced by the heroes of my own youth are similar to those facing young people today. One of my dreams has been to introduce young people to heroes who happen to be Asian Americans.

And today, with so many Americans losing their homes and jobs, these heroic struggles are an inspiration to all who fight for economic and social justice.

One of the main purposes of writing this book is to identify and honor these individuals who are heroes in the struggle for social justice. The general public does not know about the significant contributions of these individuals, and their stories have become forgotten chapters in American history and even within the Asian American experience.

Why is it that we often have a hard time identifying and giving recognition to these heroes? For Asian Americans, there are several reasons:

1. *Invisibility in the media:* One reason is that Asian Americans are often faceless, stereotyped, and invisible in the media. This invisibility can be attributed to a number of factors including racism, the lack of knowledge about our communities, and the lack of diversity in the media amongst reporters, editors, and others who make decisions about what stories or people are covered. Poor representation of Asian Americans in the mass media has largely prevented the stories and experiences of the Asian American community from reaching the general public.

2. *Invisibility in textbooks and curriculum:* While some Asian Americans have been recognized for their success in business, education, or sports, far fewer are recognized as contributors to influential political and social movements or the advancement of social jus-

tice. Asian Americans as a group have been, for the most part, absent from textbooks and curriculum taught in American schools.

3. *Difficulties in telling our stories:* Asian American communities — especially those of the immigrant or first generation — as with other newcomers and low-income communities often find it difficult or do not have the ability to promote their stories, experiences, and accomplishments. Because their stories have not been championed, many of the Asian American community's heroes are generally unrecognized and unknown even to their own.

The truth is that Asian Americans have played key roles in U.S. civil rights, labor, and human rights struggles since the 1800s and they continue on to this day. For example, Asian Americans have:

- **Fought discriminatory laws** that prohibited immigration from Asia, that banned citizenship and interracial marriages; against laws that barred Asians from owning businesses and land, and; organized against mandated segregated schools. (1880s-present)
- **Marched with African Americans** in the South in the 1960s and in the urban North, and reported on Civil Rights struggles; took stands against discrimination and violence directed at African American, Chicano and Latino, and Middle Eastern U.S. communities. (1960s-present)
- **Played a large role in organizing** farm workers, together with Mexican American labor leader Cesar Chavez. (1960s-1970s)
- **Established their own English-language** newspapers to present a fairer and more balanced picture of U.S. society to all Americans. (1940s-present)
- **Challenged laws** that violated the U.S. Constitution, especially regarding the unjust incarceration and internment of racial and ethnic groups — and eventually won vindication. (1920s-present)
- **Been a driving force** in the creation of laws against racial and gender profiling and hate-crime violence in Los Angeles and in the nation, in the years before and after 9/11. (1980s-present)

- **Organized Asian and Latino** immigrant workers against their exploitation in garment sweatshops. (1990s-present)

Untold Civil Rights Stories has been written to share with you the lives of important Asian Americans — average individuals and families who acted in extraordinary ways when caught in the midst of unusual circumstances and pressing conditions — such as anti-Asian violence, exploitation in the workplace, or unfair U.S. laws.

A second purpose for this book is to show how individuals, who are not famous, rich, or powerful, can make mighty, significant changes in their lives and for many other Americans.

Rosa Parks is often mentioned as one such ordinary person who made an extraordinary impact on the Civil Rights Movement. When we actually study the lives of ordinary people like Rosa Parks, we find that in fact, their entire lives were not so ordinary after all.

The untold civil rights stories of Asian Americans make up a hidden and vital chapter of U.S. history, and of the larger history of civil rights in this country.

As I reflect back in my own life, I know that their stories can be equally inspirational to young people so I have gathered these stories into this publication. My objective is to inspire all of us and to show role models that all of us can emulate. These individuals teach us that through advocacy that any of us, even if we are not rich, famous, or powerful, can make change.

Although there are many Asian American leaders and heroes, the following pages are devoted to those individuals with whom I have had the privilege and honor to meet. I want you, the reader to know them as I know them.

I am not the only one who was inspired and changed by these courageous heroes. The authors of these chapters have had a very significant, personal relationship with these individuals as well and I am very appreciative of their efforts to tell these stories.

A third purpose of this publication is one of education.

"The challenges faced by the heroes of my own youth are similar to those facing young people today. One of my dreams has been to introduce young people to heroes who happen to be Asian Americans."

— *Stewart Kwoh*

As I was starting law school in 1971, the 1970 U.S. Census showed only 1.4 million Asian Americans in the entire country. By 2005, that number exceeded 13 million; California alone had 4.8 million Asian Americans and Pacific Islanders. Many are immigrants from different countries arriving since 1965. They were not in the U.S. when many key laws were passed.

Would these Asians know the connection between the Civil Rights Movement of the 1960s and changes in immigration laws that affected them? Laws, policies, and practices (such as immigration quota restrictions) do directly impact minority and immigrant communities. Asian Americans, as well as all other Americans, need to know this. Americans need to know how individuals of Asian ancestry have helped to shape and influence American history and change the legal, political, cultural, and social landscape of this country.

Asian Americans even in 2009 are one of the racial groups least seen, recognized, or known on television or the news. We must challenge that state of affairs. By promoting the stories of ordinary Asian Americans whose words and actions have contributed to the Civil Rights Movement in this country, we can enhance the process of education for our fellow Americans, and for ourselves.

Moving from Invisibility

There are Asian Americans who have fought against the invisibility of Asian Americans in the media. In *Untold Stories*, I will introduce you to Beulah Ong Kwoh and K.W. Lee, both pioneers in media. Beulah Ong Kwoh was my mother and a pioneer in film and television. K.W. Lee is a journalist who continues to work to bring visibility to Asian American issues.

My mother, under the stage name Beulah Quo, challenged the invisibility of Asian Americans in film and TV. Initially she portrayed stereotypical characters but was able to move on to roles that accurately portrayed Asians and Asian Americans with great dignity and strength. Behind the camera she was also a pioneer in the production of Asian American themed plays and programs. She co-founded a theater group, the East West Players, in 1965 that provides opportunities for many minority actors.

I came to know K.W. Lee in the 1980s because he was a writer for a local newspaper that covered the Asian Pacific American Legal Center's work. I also admired his investigative reporting on cases like that of Chol Soo Lee's, a Korean American man who spent a total of 10 years in prison on a wrongful murder conviction. He brought an Asian perspective to stories in his newspapers (he published several) and the articles he wrote. K.W. helped to inform not only the Korean American community, but the community at large. After the Los Angeles riots of 1992, I was in the audience when he received the Los Angeles County Human Relations Commission Award and was amazed and proud to hear him articulate how Asian Americans and African Americans shared experiences of injustices and could build a common bond.

Ordinary Families who Organized Others against Racial Violence

I never met Vincent Chin or Joseph Ileto, who both lost their lives to racially motivated hate crimes in 1982 and in 1999, respectively. But I came to know and admire their families, who refused to allow Vincent or Joseph to remain "victims" of the media or of society. These ordinary families fought for justice and organized others against racial violence. Hate crimes, no matter when and where they take place, destroy the lives of individuals and devastate the spirit of entire communities. These two families refuse to let hate rule their lives.

I met Vincent's mother, Lily Chin, at a Detroit rally in 1983 after the killers of her son were sentenced to a mere three-year probation and a small fine.

"What can I do to help?" I remember asking her. She said, "I want justice for my son."

"The untold civil rights stories of Asian Americans make up a hidden and vital chapter of United States history, and of the larger history of civil rights in this country. As I reflect back in my own life, I know that their stories can be equally inspirational to young people."

— *Stewart Kwoh*

"Hate crimes, no matter when and where they take place, destroy the lives of individuals and devastate the spirit of entire communities."
— *Stewart Kwoh*

Photo: At a press conference right after Joseph Ileto's murder in August, 1999. From left, Stewart Kwoh, Joe Hicks, the then executive director for the L.A. City Human Relations Commission, Joel Jacinto, of Search to Involve Pilipino Americans, and Dennis Arguelles, the then executive director for the Asian Pacific Policy and Planning Council.

Although she spoke little English and rarely traveled, Lily decided that she would tour the country to get people to pressure the Justice Department to follow through. When Lily came to Los Angeles during the summer of 1984, she spoke at a crowded Chinatown restaurant. As she was speaking, she fainted. Those of us around her helped her to her feet where, despite the sweltering heat, she passionately pleaded for justice for her son. She just could not understand why her son's life was considered so insignificant that home probation and a fine were given after the perpetrators had pled guilty to manslaughter. Later that night, at my home where she was staying, I asked Lily if she was okay. She said that she had to go on; there was nothing she could do to bring back Vincent, but she did not want any other mother to go through what she had gone through.

A decade later, I found myself at the funeral of Joseph Ileto, a Filipino American postal worker who had been gunned down in a racially motivated shooting in the Los Angeles area. Joseph's brother, Ismael, and the rest of his family would become dynamic spokespersons against all forms of hate crimes, crisscrossing the U.S., speaking out and extending their hands to gays and lesbians, Jews and Muslims, and African Americans and Latinos who also were victimized. We here at APALC have come to know the Ileto family well. Their grief, anger, and concern have been transformed into visible action that has benefited all who seek to reduce the pain caused by hate. I would like you, the reader to know these two families who stood up to hate.

Understanding Injustice

There are two important lessons that I learned from Fred Korematsu, a Japanese American who resisted the government-ordered incarceration of Japanese Americans during World War II. The first lesson is that perseverance as well as courage is often required to challenge injustice. The second is that community organizations (with legal expertise) are invaluable allies.

"No understanding of U.S. history can be complete without understanding how African Americans, Native Americans, Latinos, and Asian Americans have contributed to the wealth of America through our labor."
— *Stewart Kwoh*

Fred showed uncommon courage not just once but twice, in bringing a spirited challenge to his internment. In 1942, 120,000 Japanese Americans did not have the ability to effectively challenge the U.S. government's violation of their civil rights and liberties. Even his attorney, Fred said, was himself ostracized by politically liberal organizations for representing him in his resistance to the internment order.

After a bitterly disappointing encounter with the Supreme Court, some 40 years later, Fred went back to the courts to seek vindication. Working with young attorneys at the Asian Law Caucus, Fred sought and succeeded in reversing the criminal conviction that had stigmatized him and others for decades.

Ageless Warriors

The role of the Filipino soldiers in World War II is in itself a little known chapter of American history. My Filipino American friends shared their remarkable story with me and I personally know Manong Peping, the subject of one of our chapters.

The story of Manong Faustino "Peping" Baclig is therefore an inspiring story to share with young people. A veteran of World War II, Manong Peping is now in his 80s. He is one of the key leaders of the Filipino veterans of Los Angeles. Even as a senior citizen, he remains active to a cause that is near and dear to his life.

Since the 1980s, I have worked with Filipino American organizations to propose congressional solutions to the veterans' plight and to secure health assistance for many of them in Los Angeles. So I know their fight for recognition and justice has been long. Throughout it all, Manong Peping continues to be a dynamic, articulate, and dedicated spokesperson for Filipino veterans. He seeks justice for all the Filipino veterans who served so valiantly under the command of the U.S. Army. His courageous fight serves not only Filipino veterans but all veterans who have not received the benefits that they deserve.

Understanding Our Common Experiences in the Workplace

Asian immigrants before and after World War II share a common history with other Americans… they worked in mines, on railroads, in fields, and more toiled in cities — in sweatshops, restaurants, and laundries. I would like young people to know Asian Americans who demonstrate this common history. No understanding of U.S. history can be complete without understanding how African Americans, Native Americans, Latinos, and Asian Americans have contributed to the wealth of America through our labor. Two chapters in *Untold Stories* share this history.

The United Farm Workers

In the late 1960s, when I was sitting in an Asian American Studies class at UCLA, I remember listening to a Filipino man who came into the classroom to talk about farm workers. At the time, I knew that early Asian immigrants worked on farms and in mines, and helped to drain and clear the swamplands of California. I knew that Chinese, Japanese, and Filipinos labored in the orchards and fields of the Central and the Imperial Valleys, and cast their nets from Monterey to Baja, helping to establish the fishing industries. I also knew about labor leader Cesar Chavez and the United Farm Workers Union and their mass organization.

What I did not know was that Philip Vera Cruz, the man speaking in front of me, helped to start the United Farm Workers Union. In fact, only a few of us knew that it was the energy and courage of Filipino American farm workers, who became organizers, that actually began the Union. My lesson about Asian American labor, sitting in that class, had just begun. I hope that by reading Philip's story, you too will come to know the role played by Filipino Americans in the unionization of farm workers.

Asian and Latino Sweatshop Workers in Los Angeles

Working in the garment industry is an experience many families share. It is one of the most labor intensive but poorly paid occupations. My most vivid confirmation of this fact came with a phone call.

In August 1995, I got a phone call from a neighbor who worked for a state labor agency. He asked if I could find some Thai interpreters to accompany him on a labor raid. With Julie Su, then a new staff attorney and now the litigation director at APALC, we recruited a Thai speaker who assisted, along with others from the Thai Community Development Center. Later that afternoon she told me that the labor raid had uncovered a sweatshop where more than 70 Thai workers, mostly women, had been held captive for up to seven years and forced to sew clothes.

In this book, we will introduce you to Jang, Jim, and Kaew, three Thai women who represent those enslaved in that sweatshop. They were uneducated and spoke no English, yet they stood up to some of the biggest names in the garment industry.

This raid led to a five-year struggle for liberation and justice, changing the landscape in the fight against sweatshops and justice for immigrant workers. It was their persistence, courage, and willingness to speak out and organize for themselves and with other sweatshop workers, both Asian and Latino, that secured victory for the garment workers.

I hope that *Untold Civil Rights Stories: Asian Americans Speak Out for Justice*, a joint co-publication of the Asian Pacific American Legal Center and the UCLA Asian American Studies Center, can help to educate and inspire all who read it.

My co-editor Russell Leong adds a vital link for the readers by covering the experiences of heroes within the Asian American community after the terrorist attacks of September 11, 2001. Readers are encouraged to become involved with the issues that may directly impact their lives.

I hope that young people will come to know these heroes. To encourage teachers to share these stories, I've asked Esther Taira, a 36-year veteran educator of the Los Angeles Unified School District, to develop a series of lesson plans for teachers. The lesson plans and accompanying timeline are designed to be user-friendly and encourage teachers to bring these stories to the classroom.

In addition, Irene Lee brings a young person's perspective while sharing with students her thoughtful insights as she read the chapters. There is a sense of pride and admiration in the accomplishments of ordinary people that translates into a call to personal involvement and action.

Dedication

We are all a part of a similar struggle for social justice and equality. It is through the inspirational stories of these courageous individuals that we all can be empowered to be leaders in making social justice a reality for all individuals.

Los Angeles, 2009

Chapter 1

Workers for Justice Today

"I had to work from the moment I woke up until after midnight and I had no way out. There was barbed wire, there was a guard, there were boards on all the windows. We were prisoners living in constant fear, not knowing when it would end."

—*Buppha Chaemchoi*

. . . .

"My life within the union, my life now outside the union, are all one: my continual struggle to improve my life and the lives of my fellow workers. But our struggle never stops."

—*Philip Vera Cruz*

Photo: El Monte sweatshop, Los Angeles, California, 1995. Razor wire along the back and side fence kept workers from escaping. Photo courtesy of Phil Bonner, U.S. Immigration and Naturalization Service.

Freeing Ourselves From Prison Sweatshops: Thai Garment Workers Speak Out

Julie Su

Turning My Life Upside Down

Attorneys often say that you never forget your first big case. For me, that could not be more true. As a young civil rights attorney, taking on the case of the Thai garment workers who were imprisoned in an apartment-turned-sweatshop turned my life upside down and changed me forever. I was a year out of law school and living my dream of bringing my education home to Los Angeles to fight for and alongside low-wage workers.

In 1995, when news broke of 72 garment workers from Thailand who were forced to work behind barbed wire and under armed guard in an apartment complex in L.A., I joined the team of Asian American activists who would fight for their freedom. I became the workers' attorney. Little did I know then that, beyond becoming my clients, they would also become my teachers, my friends, my sisters and brothers.

"I had to work from the moment I woke up until after midnight and I had no way out. There was barbed wire, there was a guard, there were boards on all the windows. We were prisoners living in constant fear, not knowing when it would end."

– Buppha "Kaew" Chaemchoi

When we at the Asian Pacific American Legal Center took on their case, we advocated for their freedom, fought to get them legal immigration status, and sued for corporate responsibility in the garment industry. Many told us not to do it, that the battle would take too long and that we would never win. But what they did not anticipate was the strength, intelligence, and irrepressible will of the workers themselves. Many contributed to our collective victory: countless community activists, volunteers, interpreters, students, English teachers, counselors, organizers, sympathetic government officials, reporters, and attorneys.

Movements are built by many people, and battles take time, patience, and practice to win. Throughout our work together, I was awed by the determination, the strength, the generosity, and spirit of the workers. I have had the tremendous fortune of sharing my work and life with them. Each has her own story to tell. I've learned more than I ever could have imagined from them, and so here, I share their heroic story.

Sweatshop Prisoners

August 2, 1995. Before the sun rose on another hot summer day in Southern California, federal and state law enforcement officials raided an apartment complex in El Monte, a suburb of Los Angeles. Seventy-two garment workers from Thailand were sleeping on mats on the floor, crowded eight to ten in a bedroom and held against their will. The workers' captors — a family led by an elderly Thai woman and her sons — were also captured and taken into federal custody.

Working conditions were deplorable. The workers were paid less than a dollar an hour. They were handed their wages in cash, but only after half of what they earned was deducted for travel expenses and another portion for house bills and use of the kitchen. They used what was left to buy food and other necessities from a commissary in the apartment complex run by their captors. Toothpaste, soap, fruits and vegetables were among the few items available and were sold at inflated prices. The workers had no choice but to pay.

Hundreds of thousands of pieces of cloth, spools of thread, and endless stitches consumed the daily lives of these workers. Labels of brand name manufacturers and nationwide retailers entered the El Monte apartment in boxes and left on blouses, shorts, shirts and dresses. The workers began working each day by 7 a.m., stopped briefly for lunch and dinner, and then continued working until midnight or 1 a.m.

Throughout the years, a few Thai workers managed to escape, but they were so frightened and ashamed that they dared not tell anyone.

Three Women Workers: Jang, Jim, and Kaew

Jang, Jim, and Kaew are three women garment workers from different regions in Thailand. These are their stories.

JANG: As a young girl in Nakhornsawan, a southern province of Thailand, Suchadal Eiampol lived with her parents and two brothers. Her family was poor and worked in the fields growing rice. Suchadal, who goes mostly by her nickname "Jang" loved to learn and go to school. One morning when she was

Photo: *Thai garment workers await their fate after the raid on the El Monte sweatshop by federal and state law enforcement officials in 1995.*

nine, she dressed for school as usual and waited by the door for her parents. But that day, her parents told her she could no longer go to school. She had to take care of her younger brother so that her mom and dad could both work to make enough money to feed their family. Jang was devastated and refused to take off her school clothes. In July 1992, when Jang was 28 years old, she received an offer that would change her life. A man named Sukit approached her with promises of a good job and decent wages in the United States.

JIM: It was a relatively easy decision for Sirilak Charasri, or "Jim" to leave Thailand for the U.S. She knew that she would be able to make more money for her parents, siblings and their families.

In July 1993, Jim left everyone and everything she knew to board an airplane for the first time. She was so excited she could hardly sit still. She was certain that this opportunity would turn her fortunes around because, as she says, "I thought everything about America was good." The sheer size of the country made her believe that anything was possible.

KAEW: In Thailand, Buppha Chaemechoi, her parents and three younger brothers, and her dog Pepsi shared a one room house with her grandmother in the rural, northeast province of Chaiyaphum. Like Jang and Jim, her position as eldest daughter carried with it the responsibility to care for the rest of the family. After assisting her parents with farm

work, Buppha, who goes by "Kaew," began working outside the home at age 16, mixing cement at different construction sites. Soon the pay became too low to contribute to the needs of her three younger brothers, so Kaew went to Bangkok in search of more work. She washed dishes, ran errands, and, when she was 18 years old, began sewing garments in a factory in the Thai capital. In June 1994, Kaew was only 23 years old when she arrived in the U.S.

Detention: A New Kind of Prison

Immediately after the raid in August 1995, the workers were dressed in orange prison jumpsuits, their few belongings taken from them, and free access to the outside world denied — again. This time, however, their captor was the United States government. The workers were treated as if they would be punished for the years of slave labor they had endured.

Immediately after the workers were taken into custody, attorneys and community activists rallied to fight for their freedom and tried to gain access to them to inform them of their rights. After nine days of imprisonment at the hands of the Immigration and Naturalization Service (INS) (now the United States Immigration and Customs Enforcement), community activists — including non-profit organizations such as the Thai Community Development Center,

Korean Immigrant Workers Alliance (now the Koreatown Immigrant Workers Alliance), Asian Pacific American Legal Center, and Coalition for Humane Immigrant Rights of Los Angeles, with help from UNITE, the garment workers' union, succeeded in securing the workers' freedom. These Asian American and immigrants' rights organizations were relatively small, but the staff were passionate and determined and willing to work around the clock to see the workers freed. The advocates fought for and won temporary work permits for the workers so they could find jobs and support themselves.

Because they had arrived as tourists, arranged by their captors as part of the criminal operation, all of the workers were subject to deportation once the El Monte sweatshop was raided. Initially, the U.S. government kept them in the country to serve as witnesses in the criminal prosecution against their captors.

Once the criminal case was over, many believed that they would be deported. Instead, the workers and their attorneys fought to allow them to stay. Their attorneys flew to Washington, D.C., to explore different immigration options with Department of Justice officials, high-ranking U.S. officials, INS representatives, and elected members of Congress. No one had ever used a relatively new federal law known as the S-visa to protect workers before. The S-visa, meant to protect witnesses who provide critical testimony in a criminal proceeding and are at risk for retaliation if returned to their home countries, seemed a perfect vehicle for preventing the garment workers' deportation. The workers' attorneys would spend over four years convincing the government to secure the workers' legal status in the U.S. The creative application of the S-visa in this case expanded the law beyond its original intent and created the model for new federal legislation that would greatly enhance protections for immigrant victims of violent crimes, including trafficking and domestic violence, by giving such survivors a means of staying in the U.S.

Finding New Lives

Once out of INS detention, the workers still struggled to live decent lives. Led tirelessly by the Thai Community Development Center and working together as part of the statewide coalition Sweatshop Watch, the activists met the challenge of finding affordable housing easily accessible by public transportation and in close proximity to available jobs since it would be almost a year before any of them had cars. Because the workers' health issues had been ignored in the El Monte complex, medical care and basic life skills training were also provided.

One of the toughest challenges was finding workers jobs where they would be paid legal wages and work under humane conditions. The exploitative nature of the garment industry made it difficult to find decent jobs. Several workers were placed in a union shop, but the majority returned to jobs that left them working long hours at poverty wages.

> *"When the raid happened, it seemed like we were being freed. Instead, we were thrown in prison again."*
>
> – *Suchadal "Jang" Eiampol*

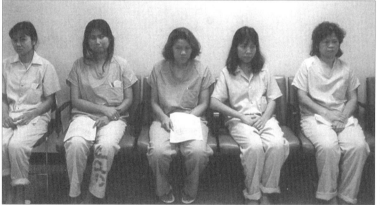

PHOTO: BOB CAREY / THE LOS ANGELES TIMES

Photo: Some of the workers under federal custody in downtown Los Angeles immediately following the August 1995 raid.

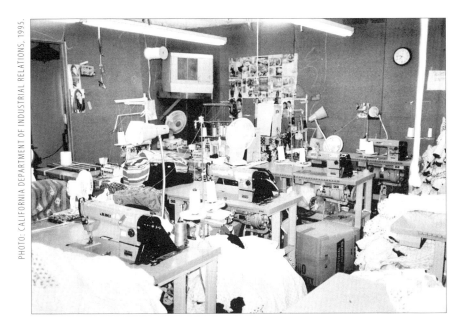

"When I got on the plane to come to America, I was so excited. America was the land of dreams. I wanted to work hard and better myself, give my family a better life, and I wanted to see this beautiful country."

– Sirilak "Jim" Charasri

Photo: El Monte sewing room, Los Angeles, California, 1995. The El Monte sweatshop operators used the first floor rooms of the apartment complex for sewing operations.

The First Federal Lawsuit

The workers, who came from impoverished areas of Thailand, were overwhelmingly women, did not speak English, and had minimal formal education. Nonetheless, they would not remain faceless. Instead, they fought back, demanding access to a legal system that too seldom hears cries for justice from the disenfranchised.

The Thai garment workers' lawsuit was the first federal lawsuit of its kind. It was about not just getting the workers paid for their long, hard labor, it was about challenging an entire industry that created the conditions for their abuse. We sued the individuals who held them captive, but also the large companies who owned the labels and sold the clothes.

The workers' lawsuit questioned whether those who are at the top of the garment industry pyramid could claim ignorance of the substandard conditions under which their garments are made. Garment manufacturers and retailers routinely try to insulate themselves from legal responsibility for the sweatshop conditions they demand and perpetuate by claiming that garment workers are not their employees. Historically, laws supporting big business and consumers have been much more common than laws seeking to hold the practices of business accountable for injustice. As a result of the efforts of community activists, civil rights attorneys, and most importantly, the workers themselves, the California State Legislature passed Assembly Bill 633. AB 633 went into effect in 2000. The bill made manufacturers and retailers responsible for garment workers' wages when their contractors fail to pay.

The Thai workers joined forces with a group of Latino garment workers who toiled in the same deplorable working conditions. The Latino workers put their jobs on the line to testify against the corporations. In a world in which poor, non-English speaking immigrants are expected to endure the huge, often alienating and lonely world in which they find themselves and to accept exploitation as the price of the American Dream, the workers defied the odds and fought back.

Retailers — Top of the Pyramid

The garment industry is structured like a pyramid. At the top of the pyramid are the retailers that sell brand name clothing directly to the public. Approximately $30 billion of California-made clothing is sold each year. This pyramid exists to shield the companies at the top from direct responsibility for wages and working conditions. Garments made by Jim, Jang, and Kaew ended up on the racks of department stores nationwide.

"When we were held against our will, we were treated like animals trapped in a cage. We wanted people to know, and we demanded that the companies know, that we are human."

– Sirilak "Jim" Charasri

Manufacturers — Second Level of the Pyramid

At the second level are manufacturers that design garments, select material, and create detailed specifications as to how those garments should be produced. These companies are more popularly known by the labels on clothing, such as Liz Claiborne, DKNY, XOXO. In El Monte, Clio, High Sierra, B. U. M., Anchor Blue, and Airtime were among those labels for which Jim, Jang and Kaew sewed.

Contractors — Third Level of the Pyramid

Contractors occupy the third level of the industry. Competition among contractors is fierce, and many open up and go out of business within a year. Contractors are at the mercy of manufacturers and retailers, which dictate the quantity, quality, type of work, turnaround times and even the prices they will pay to have that work done.

Contractors serve only one purpose — to keep the workers in line and thereby ensure that garments are completed on time and to specification. In the case of Jim, Jang and Kaew, their captors were contractors doing work for private labels sold at major department stores, including Mervyn's, Montgomery Ward and Miller's Outpost.

Garment Workers — Bottom of the Pyramid

At the very bottom of the pyramid are garment workers, who are greatest in number and lowest in economic and political power. California has an estimated 60,000 to 80,000 garment workers. Abuse of workers, including overtime pay violations, failure to pay minimum wage, and health and safety violations, is rampant.

Asians and Latinos Join Together Against Sweatshops

Jim, Jang, Kaew and the other Thai workers were not the only victims of the manufacturers and retailers who demanded garments from the sweatshop operators. Latina and Latino workers were also victimized. Though they were not held against their will, they toiled long hours, seven days a week, for below minimum wages in unsanitary conditions. The Los Angeles factories served as the "front shop" for the El Monte slave sweatshop. Manufacturer and retailer representatives routinely visited these "front shops," where Latino workers did the ironing, finish-

Retail Stores — Retail stores sell billions in clothing

Brands — Brands sell and distribute finished garments to retailers. Often design, advertise and deliver clothing.

Factory Owners — Brands hire factory owners to make their clothing. Factory owners oversee garment workers who sew parts of textiles into garments.

Garment Workers — The persons who sew the shirts/garments

Pyramid of Power and Profit
Adapted from Sweatshop Watch, 2005

ing, checking and packaging of the garments sewn by the Thai workers at the El Monte sweatshop. The Latino workers sewed under the threat of the constant barrage of screams to "work faster!"

These downtown factories, with fewer than 10 sewing machines among them during all of 1995, could not possibly have produced the volume and quantity of garments in the time demanded by the manufacturers and retailers. The quality control representatives sent by the manufacturers and retailers to monitor the sewing either knew or should have known that the orders they were giving to the sweatshop operators could not possibly have been filled at these downtown factories. Had they acted responsibly, the El Monte apartment complex would have been uncovered, and the workers' suffering would have ended much sooner.

The 22 Latino workers in the downtown location saw the quality control representatives regularly. A handful of Latino workers were responsible for loading bundles of cut cloth onto the van that brought the Thai workers their endless supply of work. Soon after the Thai workers' lawsuit was filed, a few Latino workers approached the Asian Pacific American Legal Center. The Latino workers were interested in joining the lawsuit, but they were initially distrustful of the Asian American attorneys they met. In their experience, Asian Americans often looked down on Latino workers.

This distrust was exacerbated by government agencies, the media, and the structure of the industry itself, which differentiated the workers along racial lines. The media resisted coverage of the joint effort of Asian and Latino workers, all but ignoring the Latino workers' involvement. Governmental entities followed suit, privileging the Thai workers, whose tragic story made them more sympathetic.

When the Latino workers joined the fight, the workers were also divided and distrustful of one another. In the garment industry, Asian and Latino workers often labor side by side but view one another with suspicion and hostility. Asian and Latino workers compete for poverty wages at the bottom of a multibillion dollar industry. Because they are predominantly recent immigrants, they do not speak the same language, which exacerbates tensions created by the oppressive environment they are forced to endure. The alliance formed between Jim, Jang, Kaew, and the other Thai workers and the Latino workers in this case demonstrates, that, while this racial divi-

sion can be a byproduct of the industry, it is hardly inevitable. Asian American attorneys, speaking Spanish and treating the Latino workers with respect and as comrades, also helped to bridge the divide.

As these workers found, their shared position in an industry that profits from their labor gives them a common ground on which to stand. Again defying expectations, the Thai and Latino workers joined in their lawsuit and in their broader campaign against the manufacturers and retailers, and found that their solidarity brought them tremendous power. Whether it was in the courtroom or on a picket line in front of a department store, the more workers stood together, the less vulnerable each felt. Although their fears were very real — fear of losing their jobs, fear of being labeled a troublemaker, or fear of government reprisal and deportation for becoming too visible — they drew strength from the knowledge that others were also willing to take the same risks.

At joint meetings and social events, the Thai workers learned to say "hello" in Spanish and the Latino workers came to use the "Y" symbol of respect (hands pressed together as if in prayer) in Thai greetings. They danced together to Spanish, Thai, and English songs at their annual gathering, held each August to commemorate the day the Thai workers were freed. As their attorneys and advocates, we at the Asian Pa-

"During our case, we had many meetings and we made many decisions. Our attorney wanted us to be in charge, so we worked hard and challenged ourselves and rose to the challenge."

– Buppha "Kaew" Chaemchoi

cific American Legal Center were both proud and humbled to be a part of this unlikely, powerful coming together of people willing to take risks not only for themselves, but for each other.

Using the Law, Uniting with Others

The Asian Pacific American Legal Center talked to the workers about the possibility of using the law to try and collect the millions of dollars in back wages and other damages to which the workers were entitled.

In October 1995, the workers filed an historic lawsuit in federal court against not only their captors, but also the manufacturers and retailers for which they had sewn.

Jim, Jang, and Kaew's lawsuit struck at the heart of the garment pyramid and the existing power structure. The workers' lawsuit questioned whether those who control the garment production chain could legally ignore the conditions in which their garments are made. The lawsuit also argued that the corporations should be held responsible for the sweatshop conditions they perpetuated, and from which they profited.

But the lawsuit was important for a different reason. The power that the corporations have comes from the assumption that workers have neither the will nor the ability to demand better working conditions. Workers are expected to keep their heads down and know their place. Jim, Jang, Kaew, and the other garment workers defied this assumption. They stood together and found not only their own individual voices, but a collective voice that made the simple but bold statement: "We are human."

Victory of Asian and Latino Workers United

Six months after the Latino workers joined the lawsuit, several of the companies agreed to settle. The settlement money, distributed among all of the workers, enabled them to open bank accounts, create some savings and, most importantly, send more money home to families in Thailand, Mexico, Guatemala, and El Salvador. Over the next two years, all but one company settled. After initially insisting that they had no connection to the El Monte sweatshop and no responsibility to the workers who made their clothes, the companies' payments to the workers were considered a major victory even though they did not admit fault.

In 1998, only one defendant, a company called Tomato Inc., remained. The company wanted to depose all of the workers, a total of 102 depositions. This meant the workers would be questioned under oath, every word recorded. Day after day, week after week, the workers appeared for their depositions.

Immediately following the depositions, the final company agreed to pay $1.2 million. The company also acknowledged in the settlement "the serious injustices and harms caused to garment workers by manufacturers who use sweatshop contractors. The violations of state and federal safety, minimum wage and overtime laws in garment sweatshops result in exploitation of low wage workers."

The case took nearly four years. Total settlement exceeded $4 million. Yet, the most radical changes would not be measured in dollars. The most profound changes were personal: workers standing up, speaking out, and finding their voices. Jim, Jang, and Kaew understood that the lawsuit would not provide all the solutions to the issues they faced and was just one component of a larger movement. Their strength and resilience paved the way for anti-sweatshop legislation in California, Assembly Bill 633. This case became the focal point of an exhibit at the Smithsonian National Museum of American History on sweatshops from 1820 to the present. The Thai and Latino workers in this case continued to be recognized as inspiring multiple campaigns by garment workers, college students, consumers, and other ordinary people demanding that manufacturers and retailers end the sweatshop abuses they have created in the garment industry. Though their case is over, their legacy continues.

PHOTOS COURTESY OF JULIE SU

Photo: top left, Thai and Latino workers take a break from their jobs and their activism to attend APALC's annual dinner together, October 1997. Right, Jim, Julie and Kaew at the Pride Celebration in Indianapolis, June 2008.

PHOTO CREDIT: APALC NEWSLETTER, FALL 2005 VOL. 22, No. 2.

In 2005, the Thai workers came together to commemorate their long struggle and victory. The majority of the workers remain in Los Angeles and work in garment, massage, and other industries while some have opened their own businesses. Many have married and started families of their own. The group remains tight-knit to this day.

Postscript

In August 2008, Kaew was interviewed for a front page *Los Angeles Times* article titled, "Home of the Freed." The article celebrated dozens of the Thai workers becoming United States citizens. Thirteen years after their harrowing ordeal was exposed and captured international attention, Kaew and her friends celebrated their journey at the annual Freedom Celebration hosted by the Asian Pacific American Legal Center and marked this special year with a citizenship ceremony. Surrounded by family and friends, including many volunteers who had reached out to them when their case began in 1995, the Thai workers were given American flags and hugged each other. Their story is part of a long history of individuals and communities who have fought for citizenship and belonging in a country marked by slavery and exclusion as well as opportunity and shelter. Their own place in this country was far from secure from the moment they arrived and Jim, Jang, and Kaew responded by paving a new path, a path they have now opened for others. They and the rest of the Thai and Latino workers continue a proud tradition of "outsiders" who not only make America home but challenge it to live up to its own ideals.

During the citizenship ceremony, Jim reached for her American flag, brought it to her face, and kissed it.

Photo: Jerry Whipple (center), regional director for UAW Region 6, presents a $100,000 check to the UFW executive board at a ceremony in Los Angeles in 1974. From left to right: Marshall Ganz, Eliseo Medina, Pete Velasco, Mack Lyons, Jerry Whipple, Richard Chavez, Cesar Chavez, Gil Padilla, Phillip Vera Cruz, Dolores Huerta.
Photo courtesy of El Malcriado staff.

United Farm Workers (UFW) Movement: Philip Vera Cruz, Unsung Hero

Kent Wong

What I learned from Philip Vera Cruz

I first met Philip Vera Cruz when I was an undergraduate at UC Berkeley in the early 1970s. I remember thinking how out of place Philip looked on campus. He wore old work clothes, a sweater vest, and a crumpled brown hat. His hair was gray and his face lined from the years he had worked in the fields of California under the relentless sun.

Philip had come to UC Berkeley to speak before an Asian American Studies class. When he opened his mouth to speak, the students were in for a surprise. Despite the quiet demeanor usually associated with older Asian immigrants, Philip spoke with great force and passion. Philip was a vice president of the United Farm Workers Union, the highest-ranking Filipino in the union.

"My life within the union, my life now outside the union, are all one: my continual struggle to improve my life and the lives of my fellow workers. But our struggle never stops."

– Philip Vera Cruz

Although I was active with the United Farm Workers, Philip had to teach me that it was the Filipino Americans who first organized a farmworkers union in the San Joaquin Valley. He proudly shared the story of how the Filipino Americans launched the historic Delano grape strike. He explained that the establishment of the United Farm Workers Union was a merger between two separate unions, one representing Filipino American workers and the other with a primarily Mexican membership.

Philip was a courageous union leader who dared to speak up, organize, and challenge the arrogance of power. He was convinced that although the wealthy growers, politicians, and the courts opposed the union, the workers could prevail if they stood up and organized.

Through the years as I became more involved in the labor movement, I kept in touch with Philip, and we became good friends. When I began traveling across the country to organize the Asian Pacific American Labor Alliance (APALA), Philip was always there to give me advice and counsel. The formation of APALA was a dream-come-true for Philip. For so long he had been discouraged because the contributions and potential of Asian American workers in the labor movement had gone unrecognized.

In 1991 when I began work as director of the UCLA Center for Labor Research and Education, I helped to publish a book on Philip's life written by Craig Scharlin and Lilia Villanueva. In 1992 when I was elected president of the Asian Pacific American Labor Alliance, we honored Philip as an "Asian Pacific American Labor Pioneer" at the founding convention. When my second son was born in 1993, my wife and I chose "Philip" as his middle name, in honor of Philip Vera Cruz. And in 1994 when Philip passed away, I organized a memorial service in his hometown of Bakersfield, California, and presented his eulogy.

The Delano Grape Strike and the Role of Philip Vera Cruz

The Delano grape strike in California, which began in 1965, led to the birth of the United Farm Workers Union (UFW). The strike established the reputation of Cesar Chavez nationally and worldwide.

But few people know that it was in fact Filipino American workers, under the leadership of Philip Vera Cruz and others, who on September 8, 1965, voted to strike and therefore helped to begin this historic movement in American labor. The Filipino American members voted to strike to oppose the growers' threat to reduce wages. The Delano grape strike did not end until the UFW finally won contracts with the growers in 1970.

With little formal education or training, Philip emerged as a leader of the United Farm Workers Union, a leader in the Filipino American community, and as an Asian American labor pioneer. Philip saw the farmworkers movement in a broad context as a struggle against racism, worker exploitation, and a system that is driven by profits.

The story of Philip represents a chapter of U.S. labor history and Asian American history that has seldom been told. Philip's story embodies the spirit of the *manong*, the first Filipino Americans, and the spirit of all workers struggling for liberation.

How Filipino American Workers Reached America

"When my mother asked me how long I planned to stay away, I told her three years. Well, I've been here in the U.S. over 50 years now and I haven't been back yet…"

–Philip Vera Cruz

Philip's life is part of the story of the *manong* generation, the first wave of Filipino immigrants who came to the United States in the 1920s and the 1930s to seek a better life. Almost all were young, single men. They worked in the fields, in the factories, and in low-wage service jobs.

1920s The large influx of Filipino workers began in 1924, following the passage of a restrictive immigration act that barred immigration from China and Japan. In the West Coast, the demand for low-wage laborers was filled by immigrant Filipinos. Filipinos were exempt from the racially restrictive immigration policies because the Philippines was a U.S. protectorate, and Filipinos were classified as U.S. nationals. By 1930 about one hundred thousand Filipinos were living in Hawaii and the U.S. mainland.

1930s In 1934 U.S Congress passed the Tydings McDuffie Independence Act. This act granted the Phillipines independence and changed Filipinos' status from U.S. nationals to aliens. As a result, Filipinos were subject to the same Asian exclusion acts previously imposed on other Asian immigrants. The Tydings McDuffie Act reduced the influx of Filipino immigrants from a steady flow to a slow trickle.

Life in America was harsh for the *manongs*. They found work in the most physically demanding jobs, with substandard pay and working conditions. In addition they were subjected to intense prejudice and discrimination. In the 1930s, anti-Filipino riots perpetrated by white vigilantes were common throughout the state of California.

Filipino Americans were also subjected to antimiscegenation laws that prohibited men from marrying outside their ethnic group. Due to the much lower number of Filipino women than men in the United States and the restrictions prohibiting future Filipino immigration, the *manong* generation was effectively prevented from marrying or raising families. Most lived their entire lives as single men.

His Times and Life

Philip's life, which spans almost the entire twentieth century, represents the untold story of American immigrant farmworkers from the early 1900s through the 1990s. In reflecting upon life, Philip Vera Cruz once said:

"I see life as a continuous progressive struggle — a group of people struggle to survive. They get older and they are gone. But the next ones will come together and solve some of their problems. They'll align themselves with others and make advances that the previous generation wasn't able to accomplish… If more young people could just get involved in the important issues of social justice, they would form a golden foundation for the struggle of all people to improve their lives."[1]

---

1. *Philip Vera Cruz: A Personal History of Filipino Immigrants and the Farmworkers Movement*, Craig Scharlin and Lilia Villanueva, UCLA Labor Center and UCLA Asian American Studies Center, 1992, p. 141.

An American Immigrant Farmworker

Philip was born in the Philippines on Christmas Day of 1904. His family originated in the province of Ilocos Sur on the island of Luzon north of Manila, the country's capital. In 1926, he came to the United States.

Philip said, "When my mother asked me how long I planned to stay away, I told her three years. Well, I've been here in the U.S. over 50 years now and I haven't been back yet… That's the way it has been for most of us Filipino old-timers."[2] He spent the next fifty years working in a wide variety of jobs, in a box factory in Seattle, as a busboy in Spokane, as a beet harvester in North Dakota, and as a hotel worker in Minneapolis. But most of the time, he worked as a farm laborer in California's San Joaquin Valley.

In August of 1942 during World War II, he was drafted and sent to San Luis Obispo, California, for basic training. Because he was in his late thirties, he was discharged and assigned to work on the farms in

---

2. Ibid., p. 17

the San Joaquin Valley to assist the war effort with food production.

Delano

Delano, a small town in the heart of the California Central Valley, became Philip's home. He picked grapes, harvested lettuce, and cut asparagus. During the 1940s he regularly worked nine to ten hours a day and was paid about seventy cents per hour.

Pay and working conditions in the farms were deplorable. The workers performed stooped labor in the scorching heat of the sun, where temperatures ranged from 100 degrees to 110 degrees during the summer. Farmworkers lived in labor camps with outdoor toilets, showers, and kitchens. The workers had no access to health care, no benefits, and virtually no rights on the job.

Philip said, "The facilities in those camps were pretty bad. The first camp I lived in had a kitchen that was so full of holes, flies were just coming in and out… along with mosquitoes, roaches, and everything else.

The toilet was an outhouse with the pit so filled-up it was impossible to use."[3]

The small town of Delano was divided by railroad tracks that ran north and south. These tracks also served as the color line segregating the minority farmworkers on the west side and the white farmowners on the east side. The town's business district was located on the east side of the tracks. Chinatown was located on the west side and welcomed nonwhites. The streets of Chinatown also served as the hiring hall for Filipino American grape pickers. The growers sent foremen down to the streets of Chinatown to recruit farmworkers.

The Asparagus Strike

In 1948 Philip was involved in his first strike. He went up to Byron, a small town seventeen miles north of Stockton, to work in the asparagus fields. Filipino American workers organized a strike around wages and working conditions in the labor camps.

3. Ibid., p. 5

PHOTO: GIL ORTIZ

"After all, it was the Filipinos who started this phase of the farmworkers movement when they alone sat down in Delano grape fields back in 1965."

– *Philip Vera Cruz*

"I see life as a continuous progressive struggle — a group of people struggle to survive. They get older and they are gone. But the next ones will come together and solve some of their problems. They'll align themselves with others and make advances that the previous generation wasn't able to accomplish.... If more young people could just get involved in the important issues of social justice, they would form a golden foundation for the struggle of all people to improve their lives."

– Philip Vera Cruz

The strike quickly spread throughout the Stockton area, including Byron, Elton, and Tracy. The strike was led by the Cannery Workers Union, part of the International Longshore and Warehouse Workers Union Local 37. The president of the local was Chris Mensalvas, and the Business Representative was Ernest Mangaoang, both Filipino labor leaders.

Philip said that Chris Mensalvas was the most talented Filipino American union organizer in the country in the 1940s and 1950s. Because of the labor activities of Mensalvas and Mangaoang, the government tried to deport them to the Philippines under the McCarran Act, claiming they were aliens and communist agitators. Mensalvas and Mangaoang won the case against the government after the U.S. Supreme Court ruled in *Mangaoang v. Boyd* that Filipinos who entered this country before the Tydings McDuffie Act entered as nationals and therefore could not be deported as aliens.[4]

The asparagus strike was an important milestone in Filipino American labor history. After several months, the strike won some concessions. Although the settlement was not a complete victory, this was nevertheless a significant campaign and one of the first successful strikes involving farmworkers. Many Filipino American workers, who received their first education in the power of the strike, subsequently became union leaders themselves.

1950s: Organizing Farm Workers

In the late 1950s Philip joined the National Farm Labor Union (NFLU), affiliated with the AFL-CIO. The membership was mostly Filipino Americans, with some Mexican Americans and African American workers. Philip served as president of the local in Delano. This was Philip's first experience as a union leader and the beginning of a new phase of his life.

The work to organize farm labor in the Central Valley attracted the attention of the AFL-CIO. In 1959 the AFL-CIO established the Agricultural Workers Organizing Committee (AWOC) as a pre-union formation to test the waters for farm labor organizing. Two of the first organizers hired by AWOC were Dolores Huerta and Larry Itliong. Dolores Huerta later left AWOC to work for Cesar Chavez with the National Farm Workers Association (NFWA).

1960s: Delano Grape Strike

Philip also joined AWOC shortly before the Delano grape strike of 1965. The origins of the Delano grape strike began further south in Coachella and spread north to Delano. In Coachella the Filipino workers in AWOC had demanded $1.40 an hour, a wage increase of $0.10 per hour. This was the beginning of the harvest season, and the Coachella growers acceded to the demand. Yet when the harvest season moved north to Delano, the Delano growers refused to meet the wages paid by the growers in Coachella. This triggered outrage among the Delano farmworkers.

4. Ibid., p. 14

Photo: Philip Vera Cruz (center), Vice President of the United Farm Workers (UFW), and unidentified men at a boycott meeting, c.1970s.

Photo: United Farm Workers officials, June 10, 1976. Standing, left to right: Marshall Ganz, Phillip Vera Cruz, Richard Chavez, Pete Velasco. Sitting, left to right: Mack Lyons, Cesar Chavez, Gilbert Padilla, Eliseo Medina, Dolores Huerta.

Photo: A weakened Cesar Chavez looks apprehensive. With him are Philip Vera Cruz, Julio Hernandez and Jim Drake.

On September 8, 1965, at the Filipino Hall in Delano, the Filipino American members of AWOC met to discuss whether to accept the reduced wages proposed by the growers. Instead of settling, the Filipino American members voted to strike, one of the most significant decisions in the history of farm labor struggles in California. The strike was launched by Filipino Americans and lasted for five years. In the coming years, the Delano grape strike would establish the reputation of Cesar Chavez nationally and worldwide. The birth of the United Farm Workers Union occurred during the strike. The Delano grape strike did not end until the UFW finally won contracts with the growers in 1970.

In March 1966, six months after the Delano strike began, the NFWA organized a historic farmworkers march from Delano to Sacramento. Hundreds joined the march, and thousands rallied in Sacramento. The march helped to put the Delano grape strike into the national spotlight.

Following the march, the AFL-CIO encouraged a merger between AWOC and NFWA. The merger occurred in August 1966 and was supported by the vast majority of Filipino American and Mexican American farmworkers. The United Farm Workers Organizing Committee was born under the leadership of Cesar Chavez. Three Filipino Americans were included as officers in the leadership team: Larry Itliong, Andy Imutan, and Philip.

Philip said, "When the UFW came along it really changed my life. It gave me the opportunity to bring my basically philosophical and questioning nature down to earth, and apply it to real everyday issues that actually affect people's lives. As a Filipino American it gave me the opportunity to participate in the political struggles of this country."[5]

Philip was assigned to build broad-based support for the Delano grape strike. He traveled throughout the country, speaking before students, community organizations, and churches. The United Farm Workers movement captured the spirit and imagination of people everywhere. The campaign to boycott non-union grapes attracted national and international support.

Philip also recruited new UFW supporters and organizers. For many, this was their first exposure to the labor movement, and many of today's leaders received their first union training with the UFW.

Philip, like all other union staff members, re-

5. Ibid., p. 25

ceived a salary of $5 per week plus expenses for food and gas. The UFW was not a job — it was a commitment. For Philip the UFW was his family and his purpose in life.

When the strike was finally settled and when union contracts were won, one of the first projects that Cesar Chavez launched was the construction of a retirement home for Filipino farmworkers. Plans were unveiled at the United Farm Worker's first convention held in 1971. At this convention, Cesar Chavez was elected president, Dolores Huerta was elected first vice-president, and Philip was elected second vice-president, the highest-ranking Filipino officer.

1970s: Internal Conflicts within the Union

Although he invested his life building the union, Philip had some disagreements with the leadership of the United Farm Workers. One disagreement involved the union's position on undocumented workers. The UFW feared the growth of the undocumented workforce in the fields. They feared the growers' use of undocumented workers as strikebreakers, and on occasion even called the federal immigration authorities when undocumented workers appeared to cross the picket lines. Philip vehemently disagreed with this position and firmly believed that the union had a responsibility to organize all workers, regardless of their immigration status. The UFW position was an early position on organizing undocumented workers that is different now, and has been for many years.

Philip also disagreed with the leadership of the UFW on the issue of the Philippines. In the late 1970s, Filipino American activists throughout the country were mobilizing to oppose the dictatorship of Ferdinand Marcos, president of the Philippines. Philip joined other Filipino Americans in calling for an end to martial law and widespread political repression.

In 1977 Marcos invited Cesar Chavez to visit the Philippines. In spite of Philip's opposition, Chavez accepted the invitation to travel to the Philippines, where he received a special Presidential Appreciation Award. Philip thought it was contradictory for the UFW convention to oppose some repressive regimes and not the Philippines. He said, "I cannot understand why a resolution was passed to condemn the dictatorship of Nicaragua and at the same convention, to praise the dictatorship of the Philippines."[6]

6. Ibid., p. 120

Agbayani Village

One of the first accomplishments after the UFW won contracts in the fields was the construction of a retirement home for farmworkers. The retirement home was named Agbayani Village after Filipino American farmworker Paulo Agbayani, who died while on a union picket line in 1967. Agbayani Village was designed as a sixty-unit home for retired farmworkers. Each tenant was provided a private room and an adjoining bathroom. In addition there was a central kitchen, dining hall, living room, and recreation room. The entire building had central air conditioning, an unheard-of luxury for farmworkers who spent endless summers working in the fields under the relentless sun.

Construction of Agbayani Village began in April 1973. More than two thousand people were involved in building the village, nearly all volunteers. People came from all over the country and as far away as Canada, Japan, and Europe to help.

When the village opened in 1975, Philip was the UFW officer in charge of Agbayani Village. The residents were almost exclusively manongs and retired farmworkers. Although they had worked throughout their lives in the fields, most had no life savings and no family. Yet at Agbayani Village, they now had their own community and a place to call home. Over the years, college students would make a pilgrimage to Agbayani Village to help with construction projects in order to bring gifts to the manongs and to hear their stories.

"When the UFW came along it really changed my life. It gave me the opportunity to bring my basically philosophical and questioning nature down to earth, and apply it to real everyday issues that actually affect people's lives."

– Philip Vera Cruz

Philip resigned from the UFW in 1977. In the following years, Philip lived in Bakersfield, California, with Debbie Vollmer. Debbie had a private law practice in Bakersfield where she practiced criminal defense. Philip's schedule slowed down. He spent time growing vegetables in his backyard, caring for his cats, reading, and following world events. Philip also traveled to speak to student and community groups, although with less frequency than before.

In 1987, he returned home to the Philippines after more than sixty years. He was honored by President Corazon Aquino, Ninoy Aquino's widow, and was presented the Ninoy Aquino award. Ninoy Aquino was a presidential candidate in the Philippines, and was assassinated on August 21, 1983.

In 1991 the UCLA Labor Center and UCLA Asian American Studies Center published a book on Philip's life. Written by Craig Scharlin and Lilia Villanueva, the book is now in its third printing. The publication of *Philip Vera Cruz: A Personal History of Filipino Immigrants and the Farm Workers Movement* opened up a new chapter in Philip's life. Thousands of copies were distributed. Many were used in Asian American studies and labor studies classes on college campuses throughout the country, and many young people who had never heard of Philip or the history of the Filipino American Farm Workers drew inspiration from his story.

Philip again was on the speaking circuit, addressing classrooms and speaking passionately about his life with the union. He always made it a point to get to know activists personally, especially young people. He would engage in deep discussions with them, remember their names, and always express concern about their work and their plans for the future.

On May 1, 1992, Philip flew back to Washington DC to attend the founding convention of the Asian Pacific American Labor Alliance (APALA). The APALA convention staged a march on the U.S. Department of Justice to protest the acquittal of the police officers accused of beating Rodney King in Los Angeles. Philip, at age 87, was on the front lines again, marching with other Asian American workers on May Day.

On the same evening before an auditorium of five hundred people, he received an award as an Asian Pacific American Labor Pioneer. He was thrilled to participate in a convention full of Asian American union activists who were building a new labor movement, and he was also pleased to know that others were carrying on the work he had begun as a farmworker and union organizer.

Philip said, "My life within the union, my life now outside the union, are all one: my continual struggle to improve my life and the lives of my fellow workers. But our struggle never stops."[7]

Philip passed away on June 10, 1994, at the age of eighty-nine. A memorial service was held in Bakersfield, and people from throughout California drove for many hours to attend the early morning service.

7. Ibid., p. 125

Profits Enslave the World
(A poem by Philip Vera Cruz)

While still across the ocean
I heard about the USA
So thrilled by wild imagination
I left home through Manila Bay

Then on my way I thought and wondered
Alone what would the future be?
I gambled parental care and love
To search for human liberty

But beautiful bright pictures painted
Were just half of the whole story
Reflections of great wealth and power
In the land of slavery

Minorities to shanty towns, slums...
Disgraceful spots for all to see
In the enviable Garden of Eden,
Land of affluence and poverty

Since then I was a hungry stray dog,
Too busy to keep myself alive...
It seems equality and freedom
Will never be where millionaires thrive!

A lust for power causes oppression
To rob the poor to senseless greed:
The wealthy few's excessive profits
Tend to enslave the world to need.[1]

---

1. p. xi.

Chapter 2

Families Organize against Hate Crimes

"Lily Chin declared from the very beginning that she hoped that no other mother would have to feel the pain that she did, losing a child to violence and bigotry."

–Helen Zia on Lily Chin

. . . .

"I want people to remember my brother Joseph not just as a hate crime victim, but for what his name stands for: J.O.S.E.P.H.I.L.E.T.O. Join Our Struggle; Educate and Prevent Hate; Instill Love, Equality and Tolerance for Others."

–Ismael Ileto

Photo: Lily Chin speaks at a news conference in 1983 at historic Cameron House in San Francisco's Chinatown. Rev. Jesse Jackson took time from his presidential bid to show support for the national campaign to seek Justice for Vincent Chin. Pictured on stage, left to right: Henry Der, Edward Lee, Rev. Jackson, Lily Chin, Butch Wing, Helen Zia, Mabel Teng, Alan Yee.

Lily Chin: The Courage to Speak Out

HELEN ZIA

On June 19, 1982, Vincent Jen Chin and a few close friends were out on a warm summer evening in Detroit, Michigan, to celebrate his upcoming wedding with an all-American bachelor party.

The early 1980s were a time of deep economic depression, when a massive oil crisis made it difficult for people to drive big Detroit-made gas guzzling automobiles. Instead, Americans were buying smaller and fuel-efficient Japanese cars — and hundreds of thousands of autoworkers in Detroit were unemployed, losing their jobs and their homes. Many business and political leaders pointed their fingers toward the Pacific and blamed Japan, inciting racial-hatred against anyone who looked Japanese, rather than taking responsibility for their own failed policies.

"Lily Chin found the strength to speak to thousands of people at community gatherings, rallies and demonstrations across the country, and even to appear on television."

– Helen Zia on Lily Chin

At the bar where Vincent and his friends went to celebrate, two Anglo autoworkers blamed the Chinese American for Detroit's difficulties. They called Chin racial slurs. He fought back and they chased him through the streets of Detroit. When the night was over, the two Anglo men, Ronald Ebens and Michael Nitz, beat Vincent Chin to death by swinging a baseball bat to his head several times. His 400 wedding guests went to his funeral instead.

Several months later, the two men were in criminal court, waiting to receive their punishment after they were found guilty of Vincent Chin's slaying. The shocking sentence: probation and $3,000 in fines for brutally beating another human being to death. The two Anglo men didn't spend a single day in jail for their violent and deadly crime.

People everywhere were outraged that these killers got away with murder. Chinese Americans and other Asian Americans were especially angry that the court would allow a hate crime against an Asian person go unpunished. For many Chinese Americans, it was just like the frontier "justice" of the 1800s, when a white man could kill an Asian person with impunity.

Because of this injustice, many people in the Asian American community of southeastern Michigan organized a national civil rights movement to reach out to people all across America. Vincent Chin's mother, Lily Chin, an immigrant from China who spent a lifetime of hard work in restaurants, laundries and factories, became the moral conscience of this national campaign. The goal was simple: that people of Asian descent in America should be treated as full human beings, with equal justice, fairness and dignity.

The campaign eventually forced the federal government to seek a civil rights trial against the two killers — the first time the federal government ever pursued a civil rights claim on behalf of an Asian American person. Although Ebens, the one who swung the bat at Vincent's head, was found guilty in federal court, his conviction was later overturned without either killer spending a day in jail.

Lily Chin was devastated and grief-stricken after the brutal killing of her only child. When she learned that Vincent's killers would go free with only probation and fines, her heart broke again. Yet she found the strength to speak to thousands of people at community gatherings, rallies and demonstrations across the country, and even to appear on television. Often speaking through tears, Lily Chin would say, in halting English, that she didn't want any other mother to lose their child as she did.

These and many other examples of Lily Chin's bravery inspired Asian Americans of all ages and backgrounds to speak up against hate crimes in their own communities. Numerous Asian American groups all over the country organized for equal justice and against hate violence because of Lily Chin's willingness to raise her voice. An Academy Award-nominated film called *"Who Killed Vincent Chin?"* documents her role in motivating the movement against anti-Asian violence and racism.

Sadly, Lily Chin died after a long illness in 2002, twenty years after her son was killed. She did not live to see justice done for her son, but she had the love and support of the many people whose lives were touched by her. Lily Chin's sisters asked me to deliver the eulogy at her funeral. I did so with much sorrow in my heart — and with the conviction that Lily Chin's spirit continues to live on, teaching all how one person who speaks truth to power can spark a movement to change the world.

Photo: Vincent Chin, credit: © Estate of Vincent Chin.

Eulogy for Mrs. Lily Chin
June 15, 2002, William Sullivan Funeral Home,
Southfield, Michigan

If Lily Chin were to sit up right now and look at us, I know that her eyes would get wide and they would flash that special, almost mischievous, spark that she had. She'd give us a smile as wide as this room and she'd say, "Waaahhh, look at so many people here today. Why you all come and see me?" She would say, "You make my heart very happy," and then she would try to feed us all, every one of us.

Mrs. Chin was like that — friendly, warm, generous, and funny. She was a person who loved people, especially children. She was always happy to have visitors and to hear the latest news in their lives. She was very close to her large extended family and she also loved to connect to the families of the people she met. She would never fail to ask, "How's your Mama?" Or, "How's the baby?"

You could count on Mrs. Chin to tell it like it is — if she hadn't seen you in a while, she might say, with a grin, "Eh, you look like 10 pounds heavier." Or, "Oh, you look so skinny. Better eat more." Or she'd say, laughing, "Those shoes — looks like a duck."

She was very observant and sharp; she knew what was going on around her. She read the *Detroit Free Press* and the *Detroit News* — in English, of course. She also read the Chinese language newspapers. She was very up on current events. And she knew everything that was happening with her son Vincent's case.

That's how Mrs. Chin was, and I feel very blessed to have known her. Many people only saw Mrs. Chin through the media, in her terrible grief and sadness, over the tragic death and injustice of her beloved son Vincent. I also first got to know Mrs. Chin during that shocking time.

I met Mrs. Chin at a small meeting at the Golden Star Restaurant in Ferndale, where Vincent had worked nights as a waiter. It was right after Judge Charles Kaufman let Vincent's killers off with probation and a fine for their brutal hate crime.

Mrs. Chin sat in the back of the room as people discussed the legal options. Everyone could hear her sobs throughout the meeting. But then, when it was unclear what direction the community might take, Mrs. Chin stood up and said in her firm voice, "We must tell the American people this is wrong."

In that moment, everyone could feel Mrs. Chin's courage and strength. Even in her deepest personal pain, she was able to stand up and press forward. It would have been far easier for Mrs. Chin to suffer privately than to bare her raw feelings over and over again. She relived the details of her son's terrible tragedy hundreds of times, telling the story to strangers, to reporters, to television cameras, and to Phil Donahue on national TV — each time reliving the pain, all in the pursuit of that elusive thing called justice.

The Pledge of Allegiance that Mrs. Chin took so long ago when she became an American citizen contained a promise: "with liberty and justice for all." Mrs. Chin knew very well what that meant and she wasn't fighting for her son alone. She declared from the very beginning that she hoped that no other mother would have to feel the pain that she did, losing a child to violence and bigotry.

Some people call Mrs. Chin the "Rosa Parks of Asian Americans" — and she was indeed. She stood up and refused to accept what was handed to her. Her courage rang through her grief, touching all who could hear. For me and hundreds and thousands of others, it was a call heard far and wide, uniting Asian Americans and people of conscience across this country.

Her dignity, strength, and bravery stood in sharp contrast to those who said that nothing could be done, that we had to accept another 'Chinaman's chance.' Mrs. Chin stood up to show millions of Americans that something could indeed be done.

"Some people call Mrs. Chin the 'Rosa Parks of Asian Americans' — and she was indeed. She stood up and refused to accept what was handed to her."

– Helen Zia on Lily Chin

I'm sure Mrs. Chin never imagined that she would become the symbol of moral courage to a civil rights movement that would reach around the world. When she came to America in 1947 as the bride of David Bing Hing Chin, they didn't have much in material wealth. She told me stories about her life working in a small laundry with her husband in Highland Park in the 1950s. They laundered shirts for a few cents, and sometimes they were lucky if they cleared two dollars for the day. Later on, they worked in Chinese restaurants, and when her husband retired, she took a job at a factory on 11 Mile Road, where she assembled snow brushes and ice scrapers for cars.

She lived an honest life that resonated with so many other Americans. For an Asian American like me, Mrs. Chin's story struck a deep chord. Her family story could have been my story, could have been so many of our family stories — sure, different faces in different places — but it was the same struggle and the same spirit of building a life in America.

I never heard Mrs. Chin complain about her life. Not once. She wasn't a victim — she was a doer and a fighter in every way. When it came to fighting for the check at a restaurant, Mrs. Chin could get down and wrestle anyone to the ground — she was tougher than a cowpoke at rodeo. That's how Mrs. Chin was. She had a backbone of steel and a heart of gold — she was generous and giving. Now, that didn't mean she was a spendthrift, because she knew how to watch for the bargains. But she was always making gifts for other people. And could she ever knit! She could knit a vest or a sweater in a day or two — a scarf, in a blink! She was always making something to give to someone.

And then, there was food. Mrs. Chin was a wonderful cook who only used the freshest vegetables — she would even grind her own meat. In fact, she was always whipping up delicious meals for friends, families, and the lawyers and volunteers who would often stop by her house on Gardner Street in Oak Park.

Mrs. Chin was everyone's mother, grandmother, sister, auntie. She paid special attention to the small children of so many of the ACJ volunteers who were young parents back then. I think her favorite hobby was matchmaking — she was always trying to find matches for the single, unmarried people she met.

Mrs. Chin would try to show her thanks in any way she could to all of the many people who had fought for justice with her. I know Mrs. Chin would want me to say now, again and again, that she was especially grateful to people of all colors, religions, and backgrounds from all over America, and especially here in the Detroit area. She was very familiar with the groups that were there in the beginning, such as the Detroit Chinese Welfare Council, the Association of Chinese Americans, the Japanese American Citizens League, and the Detroit Chinese Church. Above all, the American Citizens for Justice held a special place in her heart. She was deeply appreciative to so many individuals and organizations that are too numerous to mention here.

By 1987, the legal cases were over and Mrs. Chin decided to move to China, it was just too sad for her to stay in America. It was a good move for her — her elderly mother was still living then, and in the last 15 years, Mrs. Chin was able to travel on tours to Europe, Australia, and in Asia. We wrote to each other and I thought I'd share a few lines from some letters she wrote to me:

1987 — *Dear Helen, how are you? I feel very well. I stopped in Hong Kong for 10 days in October went to Canton. My Mama is very happy to see me. I buy new furniture. The price is cheap. The weather is good.*

1989 — *Dear Helen, I have your letter. I am OK in Guangzhou. Canton is good. Don't worry about me, I can take care of myself. The weather is very hot. Two weeks ago I got a letter related to Vincent. Do you understand? Thank you.*

"Her dignity, strength, and bravery stood in sharp contrast to those who said that nothing could be done, that we had to accept another 'Chinaman's chance.' Mrs. Chin stood up to show millions of Americans that something could indeed be done."

– Helen Zia on Lily Chin

Photos, left: Lily Chin at the podium with Rev. Jesse Jackson looking on. Right: One of many rallies across the U.S. calling for Justice for Vincent Chin. © Estate of Vincent Chin.

> *"Lily Chin's story could have been my story, it could have been so many of our family stories — different faces and different places, but the same struggle and same spirit of building a life in America."*
>
> – Helen Zia on Lily Chin

1994 — The house in Canton had to be torn down. I moved to Hoi Ping. I got many cousins and the town looks great. I moved to a flat. The decoration is nice. I'm fine and healthy. Thanks to all and say hello to my friends.

I was able to visit her in China. We went on walks through Hoi Ping (Mandarin: Kaiping) together, and she seemed to know everybody. People would stop her to say hello, and they'd exchange news and jokes. Mrs. Chin showed me the school she helped build with the little bit of money left from Vincent's case. She also wanted to continue the scholarship in Vincent's name that is administered through ACJ. I hope you'll all donate to it and help spread the word.

Last year, Mrs. Chin came back to Michigan for medical treatment. She didn't want people to know about her illness. She fought valiantly to stay as independent as she could, and she was able to do so with the love and care of her sister Amy Lee, her niece Jenny and nephew Lewis and their families, who all watched over Mrs. Chin around the clock during these difficult months. Mrs. Chin was also able to find some spiritual peace through church. She was baptized into the Farmington Hills Chinese Bible Church last Thanksgiving, and she found a lot of comfort from Reverend Tsang and her fellow parishioners. When she couldn't take care of herself anymore, the good

people of the Farmington Hills Health Care Center came to her assistance.

If Lily Chin were to sit up right now and smile with that sparkle in her eyes, she'd say, "Waaahhh, look at so many people here today. Why you all come to see me?"

Mrs. Chin, we're here to thank you for touching our lives with your courage, your strength, your dignity, your friendship and love. We came to let you know that you didn't fight alone and that we will continue to work for justice for all. We came to give you our love and we are so glad that you are at peace now; that you are together with your husband and with your beloved son Vincent.

I know Mrs. Chin is saying to us now, "You make my heart very happy."

Postscript:

In the years since Lily Chin's death, I often think of her — especially her laughter, the way she got excited, eyes sparkling, when she was about to make a funny observation about something she had seen or heard. We had developed a close relationship over the years and long ago we decided that I should call her "Godmother." She was indeed motherly to me and others around her, always looking after other people. Knowing this about her only deepened my sense of

"I'm sure Mrs. Chin never imagined that she would become the symbol of moral courage to a civil rights movement that would reach around the world."

– Helen Zia on Lily Chin

Photo: Lily Chin, credit: © Estate of Vincent Chin.

her loss with the murder of her only child as well as the loss of grandchildren she would never enjoy.

Mrs. Chin's special caring qualities and honesty made her the kind of person whom others looked up to and were willing to follow — an inspiring leader with her courage, forthrightness, and integrity. She was so much more than a symbol of injustice and a mother's grief, which were the images that the media had captured so movingly.

One of the saddest and most difficult things I've ever done was to tell Mrs. Chin that the civil rights case was over, lost. When she heard that there were no more legal avenues to pursue, she turned to me and asked, "Helen, is there anything else we can do?" I had to answer, "No, there's nothing more with the civil rights case." Then I watched as the pain and disappointment washed over her.

There is still unfinished business in the quest for justice for Vincent Chin. After the civil rights trial was over, there was one more court case, involving the monetary loss from taking Vincent Chin's life. A civil judge assessed the killers with a sum of money liability that the killers would have to pay Lily Chin for the loss of her son.

Ronald Ebens told reporters that he would never pay Mrs. Chin as the court ordered. He soon left Michigan and moved to Henderson, Nevada, without telling the Michigan court his new location, making it possible for him to avoid paying his court-ordered obligation to Lily Chin. The convicted killer who never spent a day in jail for his vicious attack against an

Asian American has been living a comfortable life in Nevada. But Lily Chin's estate has remained open so that Ebens will never be free of his obligation to pay for the injuries caused by his hate-motivated crime.

It is also disturbing to hear the occasional voices that claim anti-Asian racism had nothing to do with Vincent's death. In addition, there have been many cases involving members of law enforcement, public officials and the media, who automatically deny that race or discrimination plays a factor when a hate crime against an Asian American occurs, even if they know little or nothing about Asian Americans. Such attitudes exist among too many people who are ignorant about the racism that Asian Americans encounter in American society. This ignorance must be overcome through education. But when authority figures with power and influence hold such views, their attitudes are harmful to Asian Americans and to the ideal of fair and equal treatment in a civil society.

For example, playwright Cherylene Lee wrote a moving play about the hate crime against Vincent Chin in her drama *Carry the Tiger to the Mountain.* It was first staged near Washington, D.C. — in a festival that had never shown an Asian American play before. For some reason, the festival organizers decided to invite Ebens' attorney to write a comment in the program notes. His attorney wrote that Vincent Chin could have been killed by striking his head on the pavement, not from Ebens pounding his head with the baseball bat — and therefore no racism was involved. Even though this commentary contained

Photo: Vincent, credit: © Estate of Vincent Chin.

"Lily Chin's bravery inspired Asian Americans of all ages and backgrounds to speak up against hate crimes in their own communities."

– Helen Zia on Lily Chin

many false statements that were contrary to the court testimony of several eyewitnesses, including two police officers, the festival organizers published it anyway. It was as though a play about the Holocaust included notes from a Holocaust denier, or a play about slavery included comments from someone who claims that lynchings never took place.

These comments in the play's program became compounded when a theater critic wrote about the play in the *Washington Post*, an influential newspaper read by many political leaders and policy makers. The critic gave the play about Vincent Chin a negative review — because, he wrote, Ebens' attorney said it was doubtful that race had anything to do with Vincent's death.

Some people continue to believe and to perpetuate the harmful notion that Asian Americans are the "model minority" that does not encounter racism, discrimination or hate crimes. This widely held stereotype has caused much damage to Asian Americans, making it difficult to get attention for the needs of Asian American communities. The stereotype that Asians in America are not targets of racial violence

certainly played a significant role in Vincent Chin's case and the fact that a judge and a jury allowed his killers to go free.

Lily Chin stood up to all of these doubters and proved them wrong. The courage and willingness of this Chinese immigrant mother to speak out, despite her grief, continues to inspire people to keep up the fight for justice, against hate and violence in all its forms. Because of her brave stand and the hard work of American Citizens for Justice and so many voices around the country, new generations of activists and advocacy organizations are still growing and evolving.

Lily Chin reminds us that there is still much to be done, and that there is a terrible price to pay if we don't speak up. Lily Chin, a dear mother who immigrated from China and spent a lifetime working in restaurants, laundries and factories so that her son could have a better life, showed us what is possible — and what we are all capable of. Her shining example of standing up and speaking out, even when it is most difficult, is an inspiration for all people who value fairness, equality and justice in society.

A Family Educates to Prevent Hate Crimes: The Case of Joseph Ileto

STEWART KWOH

I found myself at the funeral of Joseph Ileto, a Filipino American postal worker who had been gunned down in a racially motivated shooting in the greater Los Angeles area. Little did I know at the time that Joseph's brother, Ismael, and the rest of his family would become dynamic spokespersons against all forms of hate crimes, crisscrossing the U.S., speaking out and extending their hands to gays and lesbians, Jews and Muslims, and African Americans and Latinos who also were victimized.

1. Why Was Joseph Ileto a Hate Crime Victim?

On August 10, 1999, Joseph Santos Ileto, a Filipino American postal worker was gunned down along his Chatsworth route by a self-professed white supremacist named Buford O. Furrow. Just hours after Furrow fired shots into a playground full of children at the North Valley Jewish Community Center (NVJCC) in Granada Hills, the killer encountered Joseph, who happened to be covering another mail carrier's route that day.

"Why *can't* they see us?"

– The Ileto Family

urrow approached Joseph and asked him to mail a letter for him. As Joseph agreed to mail the letter, Furrow pulled out his gun and shot Joseph nine times. Furrow later confessed that he killed Joseph because he looked Latino or Asian and because he was a federal employee. Furrow also stated that Joseph's racial background and employment with the government made him a good "target of opportunity." As Joseph tried to run away, the killer shot him a few more times before finally escaping himself. Joseph died from gunshot wounds to the chest and one to the back of the head and was the only fatal victim during Furrow's rampage. The day immediately after the shootings, Furrow turned himself in to the authorities and confessed his guilt.

Kuya — Who Was Joseph Santos Ileto?

To his family, Joseph was fondly known as Jojo or *Kuya*, a Filipino term of respect for an eldest brother. With the death of their father at an early age, Joseph played a central role in the household. A filial son, a devoted brother and brother-in-law, *Kuya* was an honest and modest man who never hesitated to help others. Ismael Ileto, Joseph's younger brother, recounted an incident where Joseph helped the local sanitation workers when they came around on their shift. "That's their job," Ismael recalls saying, but that did not stop Joseph from helping those men.

At 39, things were going well in Joseph's life. While attending California Polytechnic at Pomona for an Engineering degree, Joseph went to work at the United States Postal Service. An avid chess player, Joseph had been featured occasionally in magazines and newspapers for his accomplishments. Joseph had also just become an uncle as his brother Ismael and his sister-in-law Deena celebrated the arrival of their son, Kyle. Close to his younger twin sisters Carmina and Raquel, and his loving mother Lilian, Joseph was the family's big brother, their *Kuya*, in every sense of the word.

Around the time of Joseph's death, the national media had prominently focused on the brutal hate crimes perpetrated against an African American man in Texas named James Byrd, and a gay man in Wyoming named Matthew Shepard. In the wake of these murders, the Iletos were aware that hate crimes

What is a hate crime?

The California Attorney General's Civil Rights Commission on Hate Crimes Final Report, March 2001, defines a hate crime as: "Any act of intimidation, harassment, physical force or threat of physical force directed against any person, or family, or their property or their advocate, motivated either in whole or in part by hostility to their real or perceived race, ethnic background, national origin, religious belief, sex, age, disability, or sexual orientation, with the intention of causing fear or intimidation, or to deter the free exercise or enjoyment of any rights or privileges secured by the Constitution or the laws of the United States or the State of California whether or not performed under color of law." Joseph's death falls within the scope of this definition because he was singled out and killed based on the color of his skin.

Photo: the Ileto family, seated, from left: nephew Kyle, sisters Carmina and Raquel, sister-in-law Deena and mom Lilian. Standing behind the family are, from left, Chris Komai of the Japanese American National Museum, the Hon. Judy Chu, L.A. Mayor Antonio Villaraigosa and Ismael Ileto at the APALC Commemoration Event for Joseph Ileto in August 2005.

"Before, we would watch TV thinking that hate crimes would never happen to us or, good thing, we don't live in that area."

– Deena Ileto

were happening but it never occurred to them that someone in their own family could become a victim.

"We never even got the chance to say goodbye. I want to tell him that we miss his company and I hope he can see that we're doing our best to honor his name," Ismael said, fighting back tears, "I want people to remember my brother Joseph not just as a hate crime victim, but for what his name stands for: J.O.S.E.P.H.I.L.E.T.O. Join Our Struggle; Educate and Prevent Hate; Instill Love, Equality and Tolerance for Others."

2. U.S. Media Fails to Cover Hate Crimes Against Asian Americans

As the Ileto family received the shocking news of Joseph's death that summer afternoon, coverage of a crazed lone gunman emptying bullets into a playground full of children was the lo-

cal and national media's greatest concern. Five people in the NVJCC shooting were seriously hurt and footage of young children being led out by the police were the recurring images sensationalized on television throughout the day. The brutal murder of Joseph and the shooting at NVJCC, both disturbingly violent, were reported as almost unrelated events. The murder of the Filipino American postal worker received minimal news coverage.

The media's consistent failure to adequately cover anti-Asian Pacific American (APA) incidents can explain the public's general lack of awareness of anti-APA violence. In 1999, although four racially motivated murders against Asian Americans occurred, only those that involved other religious and racial minorities such as the shooting of five at the Jewish Center along with the Joseph Ileto killing received public attention.

Civil Rights Violation Penalties

On February 6, 2003, more than three and a half years after the tragic death of Joseph, the California Fair Employment and Housing Commission ruled that Furrow violated Joseph's civil rights and caused extreme emotional distress to his family. The Commission ordered Furrow to pay $150,000 in compensatory damages and $25,000 in civil penalties to the estate of Joseph. This was the first time that the maximum penalty was awarded for a hate violence case under California's Ralph Civil Rights Act. The Commission's decision to order the maximum penalty was based on the coroner's determination that Joseph experienced tremendous emotional and physical trauma in the minutes before he died and because of the severe nature of the hate violence expressed in this case.

It is unlikely Joseph's family will receive any money from Furrow. However, the ruling is important because it sets a precedent for families of hate crime victims to get financial redress. Joseph Duff, the housing agency's senior staff counsel who presented the case, said "the ruling affirms the power of this department to bring action on behalf of victims' families. It sets a legal and social precedent that will benefit future hate crime victims in California."

Asian Pacific American victims often receive less coverage than the victims from other racial groups. To a large extent, Asian cultures deem family matters to be private and many hate crimes against those of Asian descent have gone unreported. Because it holds the power to influence public perception, the media's failure to report anti-Asian violence results in incomplete and inaccurate understandings of the nature and true extent of the problem.

Enraged to find Joseph's death being ignored, the Iletos decided to break their silence. Thus, this began the family's transition into the spotlight of anti-hate crime activism.

3. An Ordinary Family Speaks Out to Educate the Public

Ismael Ileto, Joseph's brother, became the family spokesperson in the wake of the tragedy, and continues to be a speaker against hate crimes today. However, taking on this role did not come naturally to him.

As a student at California State University, Los Angeles, Ismael Ileto was neither a political or social activist nor an outspoken speaker. Ismael had once joined a protest of the brutal Detroit hate killing of Vincent Chin, but that was the only form of activism he had participated in while in college. Furthermore, politics was not a large concern to the Iletos. Hate crimes, especially, seemed to be a distant issue for them. Ismael admitted, "For some reason, we always feel that somebody else is already doing the job. There is no need for us [to be politically and socially active]."

That all changed on August 10, 1999.

Ismael realized that he would have to be his brother's silenced voice. "We've come to realize that we have to do it for ourselves, for Joseph," Ismael said. "No one else is going to do it [hate crime awareness]." The loss of Joseph sparked a determination in the family to find the strength to speak out to others.

"Before, we would watch TV thinking that hate crimes would never happen to us or, good thing, we don't live in that area," Deena Ileto, Joseph's sister-in-law, explained. "And then it happened to us. It was shocking. You come to the realization that there is no type of area and no one is safe when hate is all around us. After Joseph's death, we realized that we needed to do something. We owed it to (Joseph)."

Experienced in dealing with tragedy in the public arena, Jewish activists promptly activated a well es-

"You shouldn't be embarrassed,
you should be *enraged*."
– Ismael Ileto

Photo: Ismael Ileto, above, fourth from left.

tablished network to rally together after the shooting spree. The Iletos, who deeply sympathized with the Jewish victims of the shooting spree, were afraid that Joseph's tragedy would be ignored. This was not just an anti-Semitic attack, it was also an anti-Asian one.

The Ileto family quickly came face to face with the invisibility that Asian Pacific American hate crime victims and their loved ones routinely experience. The family soon became frustrated, and began asking the question, "Why can't they see us?" Despite the fact that the family was invited to events and memorials where politicians and the media would express their condolences, when it came time to making public comments about the August 10th tragedy, no one mentioned Joseph or the fact that he was an APA.

4. Making Hate Crime Victims Visible

Seventeen days after the shootings, a gun control legislation bill was signed by the governor in Los Angeles. The Ileto family was invited to sit in the front row and quickly realized that there were only a handful of Asian Pacific Americans in the entire audience. Governor Gray Davis was there to sign three bills. In his speech, he addressed representatives of the Jewish community and mentioned the Jewish Center shooting numerous times, but failed to mention Joseph even once.

"As people were walking out," recalled Ismael, "Governor Davis announced, 'By the way, the Ileto family is here.'" Lilian Ileto turned to her family and

exclaimed that she was terribly embarrassed, and in a way, hoped there were no other Filipinos there to witness that her son Joseph was not acknowledged.

"You shouldn't be embarrassed, you should be enraged," Ismael recalled telling his mother. Deena remembers asking: "Why are they oblivious to us when we are sitting right in front of them?" It was as if people would only recognize the Iletos or Asian American hate victims if they stood up and made noise.

That incident at the bill signing only served to galvanize the Ileto family's quest to include Joseph and other Asian American hate victims in the national dialogue on hate crimes. Today, the Iletos spend all of their free time, vacation time, and days off dedicated to educating people about hate crimes and how to prevent them.

In the days following Joseph's murder, various civil rights and community-based organizations, together with members of the Asian Pacific American and Jewish communities, organized vigils and rallies denouncing hate-motivated violence in Los Angeles, New York, Washington, D.C., San Francisco, Chicago, Dallas, and Seattle. Within the Filipino American community, Jon Melegrito, executive director of the National Federation of Filipino American Associations (NaFFAA), said many Filipino Americans "think of themselves as model minorities who are not vulnerable to discrimination, let alone hate crimes." Prosy dela Cruz, a Filipino American organizer, further acknowledged that as a Filipino American, Joseph's death was something "you don't expect when you come to the United States to pursue the American dream." These were the exact sentiments shared by the Iletos.

In the wake of Joseph's death, Joseph's mother Lilian was terrified to speak up. She feared retaliation from White supremacists. Her fear was not unfounded. The Iletos have since received vicious hate mail and explicit, threatening phone calls. To protect themselves from danger, Ismael and Deena have moved. Because both brothers work for the mail industry, Ismael, a UPS driver, is especially traumatized by the hate mail. Yet, in spite of the obstacles they have faced, the Iletos remain committed to their cause.

Joseph's mother (Lilian), brother and sister-in-law (Ismael and Deena), and sisters (Carmina and Raquel) tirelessly marched in the streets, attended city council meetings, and rallied for stronger federal hate crime and gun control laws. In the name of Joseph, the family turned their sorrow and frustration into powerful tools of social activism making it their mission to support all victims of hate crimes, regardless of race, creed, national origin, or sexual orientation. In doing so, they have successfully built a multi-cultural coalition to promote hate crime awareness and hate crime prevention.

5. Obtaining Justice for Hate Crime Victims

"In Catholic school, we are taught to forgive and forget," Ismael said, "but it's hard when your brother's killer is smiling as he apologizes in the stand." The Iletos' only desire was for justice to be properly served on Furrow.

At a time when overt racial discrimination is rarely condoned, such hate killing is "a bitter reminder that bigotry is (still) alive," U.S. district Judge Nora Manella told the killer. Prosecutors sought the death penalty against white supremacist Furrow. With U.S.

Attorney General Janet Reno's approval, U.S. Attorney Alejandro Mayorkas filed the death penalty notice. Furrow was indicted on hate crimes in the wounding of three boys, a teenage girl, a receptionist at the North Valley Jewish Community Center and the killing of Joseph (*Asianweek.com* Jan. 5-11, 2001).

Judge Manella imposed on Furrow two life sentences without possibility of parole, 110 years in prison, and payment of $690,292 in restitution. The judge reprimanded the killer, "If you've sent a message, it is that even the most violent crimes can strengthen a community." The family expressed a sense of relief knowing that the killer would be forever kept behind bars. "Although it can't take away the sorrow and pain, or return our brother back to us, at least he is kept away from harming another person. I wouldn't want any family to go through what we went through because of him," Ismael said. Joseph's mother Lilian says her only peace of mind is that Furrow cannot harm another family again.

The brutal deaths of Joseph and other hate crime victims have helped raise the nation's consciousness regarding hate violence. The Hate Crimes Prevention Act of 1999 (HCPA) was introduced to provide more federal resources to address the problems of hate crimes.

Progress halted, however, after the September 11, 2001, terrorist attacks of the World Trade Center in New York City. This was particularly distressing for Asian Americans because of the rise in hate crimes towards South Asians immediately after September 11. Over 250 bias-motivated incidents targeting APA's have been documented and 96% of those incidents involved South Asians. Individuals in universities, workplaces, and public places have been subject to racial slurs and threats as well as physical attacks. Almost immediately after September 11, two Asian Americans, a Sikh American and a Pakistani American, were brutally murdered. While previous racially motivated assaults involved only male victims, the

"We've come to realize that we have to do it for ourselves."

– Ismael Ileto

"How many more have to die
before we're important enough...
for people to listen to our issues?"
– Ismael Ileto

Photo: the Ileto family at the APALC Commemoration Event for
Joseph Ileto held in August 2005.

current trend post September 11 include women and children as victims.

According to Intergroup Clearinghouse, a San Francisco organization, more than 1,700 cases of discrimination against Arab Americans, South Asian Americans, Muslim Americans, and Sikh Americans have been reported as of January 2002. Sikh Americans have been disproportionately targeted for the backlash post September 11 because their appearance resembles that of Arab and Muslim Americans. In California alone, hate crime offenses based on a person's race, ethnicity, or national origin, increased 21 percent in 2001 due to backlash from the September 11 attacks. (Hate Crime in California 2005, California Attorney General's office).

The inability of the federal government to address hate crimes is pressing and needs to improve quickly. The Local Law Enforcement Enhancement Act (LLEEA) of 2001 seeks to address the government's capacity to address hate crimes. Public officials and community leaders including the U.S. Attorney General must step forward to address the growing con-

cerns of such hate motivated crimes and take action against hate crimes by taking measures such as supporting funding for anti-bias educational programming. Various APA communities have been reaching out to the victims of the terrorist attacks and the victims of the backlash since September 11.

6. Tragedy to Activism: Celebrating the Bayanihan Spirit

In memory of Joseph, the Ileto family invoked the Filipino spirit of *bayanihan*, across different groups and has built a multi-racial coalition in their fight against hate crimes. Bayanihan is a traditional Filipino custom to help one another as one larger community. In their quest to speak out against hate crimes, the Ileto family has reached out to various groups that they had no prior affiliation with in a desire to build a larger community against hate crimes. They have built a coalition with a pan-ethnic identity that includes diverse groups from other Asian American communities to gay and lesbian organizations.

"Hate that stems from intolerance or ignorance is unacceptable no matter what form it takes."

– *The Ileto Family*

"We are pushing for a bill that will put criminals away for all motivations for hate crimes. For discrimination against race, gender, disability, and sexual orientation," Ismael said. One of the problems that the Iletos are facing is that many politicians are reluctant to include sexual orientation on that list. The Ileto family met with the parents of Matthew Shepard and shared their grief.

"We want a bill that covers everyone," says Ismael. "Hate that stems from intolerance or ignorance is unacceptable no matter what form it takes."

The Iletos are public supporters of the Local Law Enforcement Act (formerly the Specter-Kennedy Hate Crimes Bill). As of March 2009, this bill still has not been passed because of opposition to its inclusion of sexual orientation and/or gender related hate crimes.

Robin Toma, a civil rights attorney and the executive director of the Los Angeles County Human Relations Commission said, "I know that because of the tireless activism of the Iletos, people everywhere have been touched by their story of the devastating impact of hate crimes." Toma is like many others who strongly agree that the way the Ileto family has turned their grief into activism is astounding. "Even if they do nothing more in their lives, their willingness to speak out in favor of understanding and prevention of hate crimes has impacted millions and serves as a shining example of what human beings can be. They are personal heroes to me."

The Iletos are not solely concerned with hate crimes against Asian Pacific Americans. They have traveled near and far, accepting all invitations to speak at rallies and conventions for many different causes. Ismael explains "… the family has been going out to different campuses and colleges to bring their awareness to the students in colleges and high school students… just to make them aware that it could happen to them… we are there to tell them that, hey, we are targets. And we need to stick together… We are [also] asking the different parishes and churches and faiths to address the issue of hate crimes in their congregation… we are building bridges with other communities because that's what we need, to unite together. Because we can't just fight this alone."

The family marched with Jesse Jackson in October 1999 in support of the National Rainbow Coalition's effort to unite communities of different faiths to prevent hate crimes. Among the various local events the Iletos have participated in, the family also spoke

PHOTO COURTESY OF THE ILETO FAMILY

"I want people to remember my brother Joseph not just as a hate crime victim, but for what his name stands for: J.O.S.E.P.H.I.L.E.T.O. Join Our Struggle; Educate and Prevent Hate; Instill Love, Equality and Tolerance for Others."

– Ismael Ileto

Photo: the last picture taken of Joseph at his nephew Kyle's birth at St. Jude in Fullerton, CA.

at the National AFL-CIO Union Convention, at the Museum of Campaign as part of the Million Mom March against gun violence.

Since Joseph's death, the Iletos have become actively involved with organizations that strive to prevent hate. The Asian Pacific American Legal Center of Southern California (APALC) in Los Angeles has created the Joseph Ileto Hate Crimes Prevention Fellowship that serves as a memorial for Joseph by advancing education and advocacy around the issue of hate crimes and strengthening intercommunity networks

as a means of preventing hate crimes. The family has also been actively involved with the Filipino Civil Rights Advocates (FILCRA), a group that worked with APALC to provide support for hate crime prevention. Recognizing that brutal crimes like the hate murder of Joseph, continue to happen in our society even today, Deena feels the collaboration of various groups is especially important.

"We need to be more outspoken. How many more have to die before we're important enough... for people to listen to our issues?" Ismael asserted.

If you think you have been the victim of a hate incident or hate crime you should report it immediately to your law enforcement agency. Reporting a hate incident or hate crime to law enforcement may keep others from being victimized. It is also important for law enforcement to be aware of what is happening in their jurisdictions so they can take necessary steps and provide resources to make the community safer. Let the officer know that you think you were a victim of a hate crime or hate incident. If words were used during the incident, write down the exact words that the perpetrator used in connection with the incident and anything else that would link the perpetrator to the incident. *(safestate.org- project of the California Attorney General's Crime and Violence Prevention Center)*

Chapter 3

Crossing the Color Line and Building Racial Bridges in the Movies and in the Media

"There is this myth that Americans aren't interested in seeing a hero who happens to be an ethnic minority. That's nonsense! We have to educate the viewing public!"

–Beulah Ong Kwoh

"My small newspaper is here to chronicle their struggle, telling the untold story of our people — with warts and all — in their full human context, not only for the outsiders, but for our future generations."

–Kyung Won Lee

EAST WEST PLAYERS
TIM DANG, PRODUCING ARTISTIC DIRECTOR
PRESENTS THE WEST COAST PREMIERE OF

CARRY THE TIGER
TO THE MOUNTAIN

BY CHERYLENE LEE
DIRECTED BY TIM DANG

The epic true life story of Lily Chin,
a postwar picture bride who became
a civil rights activist following the
beating death of her son Vincent Chin.

February 24 - March 14, 1999   Telecharge 800 233 3123
EAST WEST PLAYERS
David Henry Hwang Theater at the Union Center for the Arts

Breaking the Color Line in Hollywood: Beulah Ong Kwoh, Actor

MARY ELLEN KWOH SHU AND STEWART KWOH

From Invisible to Visible

"There is this myth that Americans aren't interested in seeing a hero who happens to be an ethnic minority. That's nonsense! We have to educate the viewing public!"[1]

– Beulah Quo (stage name for Beulah Kwoh)

When we were young children growing up in Los Angeles in the 1950s, none of the faces on our television screen were yellow, brown, or black. Nobody looked like us. We were invisible on television, in films, and the mass media. In fact, not only Asian Americans, but African Americans, Native Americans, Latinos, and Chicanos were often invisible as well. If they did appear on screen, they were usually cast in predictable, stereotyped roles of houseboy, maid, laundryman, cook, gardener, or driver, or gangster.

---

1. Beulah Quo. *An Official Biography*, 1983.

"We were invisible on television, in films, and the mass media. Nobody looked like us."

— Beulah Kwoh

Fifty years later, Hollywood now has many actors of color, from Denzel Washington to Jennifer Lopez to Jackie Chan. The road from the old Hollywood to the present was not an easy one. It took the courage and dedication of many. Our very own mother, Beulah Ong Kwoh (Quo) helped to break the entrenched "color lines" of Hollywood. In her long and distinguished acting career, our mother became one of Hollywood's most respected artists, a hero to many not only for her acting ability but also for her selfless determination to see Asians portrayed fairly on the screen and stage. Her efforts and achievements helped widen the door for many others.

A Daughter of Immigrants

Beulah did not plan to become a Hollywood actor. Born on April 17, 1923 in Stockton, California, she was the only child of a Chinese immigrant couple. Her parents were very poor, and Beulah would scrub floors for five cents an hour to help make ends meet. From a young age, Beulah was taught the importance of hard work and education as a means to a better life. These values guided Beulah in her journey as a teacher, a Christian, a producer, a visionary and an activist.

After graduating Phi Beta Kappa from the University of California, Berkeley, Beulah received a Master's Degree from the University of Chicago. Around this time, she met and fell in love with a young Chinese student, Edwin Kwoh, who was completing his doctorate at Columbia University and who, like Beulah, was very active in the Chinese Christian movement. They married and, for two years, worked at a university in Nanjing, China where they hoped to help rebuild a country ravaged by war. After the Communist takeover in 1949, however, they fled back to California, bringing with them their infant son, Stewart.

An Actor Who Paved the Way

The family settled in Los Angeles and grew to include a daughter, Mary Ellen. By this time, Beulah was teaching sociology at the Los Angeles Community College and running the local church nursery school. In 1954, a friend referred Beulah to director Henry King who was working on the movie *Love Is a Many Splendored Thing* starring William Holden. King needed a dialect coach for Jennifer Jones who was to portray Han Suyin, the real-life Eurasian doctor upon whose life the movie was based. To play her part, Ms. Jones needed to speak with a British-Chinese accent. "Mr. King said that I had a California accent, but wondered if I'd be interested in acting. He thought I was ideal for the part of Miss Jones' aunt!"[2]

Recalling this serendipitous beginning of her acting career, Beulah later commented, "I had never acted before, but thought it would be fun. Instead, I fell in love with the profession as soon as I got the greasepaint on my face!"[3] At a time when many wives stayed at home while their husbands worked, Beulah received the support of her husband, Edwin, to pursue acting. "His family was less traditional than mine… in the way we Cantonese have a lot of superstitions, a lot of protocol about relationships. Edwin's family was very westernized. I never had to fight anything at home to pursue my career."[4]

Beulah continued to land other small character roles. "I kept getting jobs because in the '50s and '60s, there were a lot more movies and there were not so many young women going into acting. Since I liked

2. Ibid.
3. Quoted in Elrik Knutzen. *"Asian-American Quo Fights the Good Fight." Los Angeles Herald TV Weekly*, 1985.
4. Quoted in *"Beulah Quo: A Believer in Giving."* AAPAA's *Inside Moves*, Oct. 1982.

The East West Players gave Asian American actors a place of their own to create full and multidimensional characters rather than the flat, one-sided images of Asians commonly portrayed by Hollywood at the time.

it and felt it extended my sociology, I could do something with it. Having been a teacher you're always sort of a ham!"[5] Early in her career, Beulah changed her last name, "because I got tired of being asked, 'Is KWOH a radio station?'" To make things easier, she decided to change her stage name to "Quo."

Recognizing the need for some formal acting training, Beulah became a student of the Desilu Workshop, a theater group started by Lucille Ball for new talent. Beulah studied for three years under the guidance of director Joe Sargent, working with both Asian and non-Asian American actors. "You learn from people who've had a different background from which to pull their gut feelings. There are certain experiences that a non-Asian actor has that we can't possibly have, sometimes because their horizons are wider. Asian Americans still feel somewhat limited, self-imposed or imposed by society, especially in my

day when the restrictions were stronger."[6] There she met Jimmy Hong and Pat Li who would join Beulah as early Asian American pioneers of the film industry.

The First Asian American Theater Company

Asian American actors needed the opportunity to highlight their talents so directors and producers would cast them. In 1965, Beulah and her friends, including Mako and Soon-Tek Oh, decided to take action. They created East West Players, the country's first Asian American theater company. East West Players gave Asian American actors a place of their own to create full and multidimensional characters rather than the flat, one-sided images of Asians commonly portrayed by Hollywood at the time.

Lacking a theater of their own, these dedicated founders rehearsed and performed in the basement of

5. Ibid.

6. Ibid.

the local Presbyterian church in the Silverlake area of Los Angeles and later moved to a store front on Santa Monica Blvd. Beulah served as chair of the board of directors while Mako served as artistic director. This was an especially difficult time for the fledgling organization. According to Esther Kim Lee in her book, *A History of Asian American Theatre*, "…core members such as Beulah Quo and Rae Creevey… willingly spent their personal time and money to get through the tough times. Quo was especially indispensable during this time. Other members relied on Beulah Quo to save the company by finding financial and legal resources."[7]

Through the dedication and personal commitment of Beulah and her colleagues, the little group survived and grew during the first eight critical years. Classes were offered to aspiring and already established actors. Productions such as the classic Japanese story *Rashomon* and Federico Garcia Lorca's *House of Bernalda Alba* gave Asian actors the opportunity to hone acting skills as well as develop self-confidence by portraying non-stereotypic roles. Many of today's successful Asian American actors gained their first experiences performing in an East West production.

Importance of Breaking Media Stereotypes

Entertainment media influences the general public's view of various groups of people. Stereotype — the oversimplified standardized image or idea held by one person or group of another is all too often found in film and television. Stereotypes of ethnic minorities have portrayed them narrowly as servants, laborers, or as criminals. Negative views are supported and the fact that a wide range of differences found in any group is ignored. What are some common stereotypes you have seen?

With the establishment of this theater company, the acting community of Chinese, Japanese, Korean, and Filipino Asian Americans grew. "Beulah treated everyone like family with a warmth that connected people regardless of age, language, and ethnicity."[8] "Auntie Beulah," as she was so often called, became a vital link between many in the acting community.

Tim Dang, who later became the artistic director of East West Players, commented, "She spread her supportive advice to her extended family of artists about the entertainment business. But I think I got some special treatment from her when I became the artistic director of East West Players, the theater that she helped found in 1965. She wanted me to meet every person she knew or was just acquainted with that could help with contributing to East West Players both financially and artistically."[9]

From bringing Chinese congee soup, a traditional rice porridge dish, to sick friends to mentoring young aspiring actors, Beulah touched many lives. Reggie Lee, the young Filipino Chinese actor who portrayed Vincent Chin in the production *Carry the Tiger to the Mountain*, commented, "When I was younger, I wanted to be blond! Beulah helped me appreciate where I came from, that I am both Asian and American. She also helped me to know that I could make it in this business, too. I was fortunate to be one of her sons!"[10]

Playwright Cherylene Lee who worked with Beulah on *Carry the Tiger to the Mountain* acknowledged the influence that her long friendship with Beulah had upon her work as a writer:

"It wasn't until 1982, the year Vincent Chin was murdered, that I suddenly realized that though I've always seen myself as an American, there was a gap in how Asian Americans perceived themselves and how non-Asians saw us. I began to understand why Beulah worked so tirelessly to make Asian Americans more visible in American life. I began to write plays which explored this gap in perception and I tried to find ways in my plays to bridge the gap, to show parallels and contrasts, to use the past and the present, to acknowledge tradition and what is lost in the process of being American — themes which I continue to explore in my plays today."[11]

7. Esther Kim Lee. *A History of Asian American Theatre*, p. 49.

8. George Takei, Telephone interview, April 4, 2005.
9. Tim Dang, E-mail to author, May 20, 2005.
10. Reggie Lee, Telephone interview, May 5, 2005.
11. Cherylene Lee, E-mail to author, June 7, 2005.

PHOTO COURTESY OF AUDREY MAGAZINE

"The mission of the Association of Asian Pacific American Artists (AAPAA) was to promote more realistic and balanced images of Asians in the media and to fight against stereotyping in television and movies."

— *Beulah Kwoh*

Photo: *Above,* Beulah Kwoh as "Guard Velie" poses for the camera while shooting *Brokedown Palace* (1999).

Breaking Stereotypes and Recasting Our Roles

"Most of the time I would say they are not out to offend. It's just that they don't know. I have gone to producers several times and said, 'Look, you're going to get calls from the community on this — to say chink or Chinaman is not acceptable.' And those producers will be genuinely surprised."[12]

–Beulah Quo

Beulah observed many instances in which people of color were cast in stereotyped roles. Asian women, in particular, were portrayed, more often than not, as prostitutes, maids, and meek, subservient women. She was cast in one such role in the 1966 movie *Sand Pebbles* where she played the role of a Chinese madam named Mama Chunk.

As she began working on the film, Beulah found it frustratingly difficult to play her character because of the common, one-sided nature of the role she was portraying. This experience deeply impacted her and further strengthened her resolve to fight for a more balanced representation.

During the 1960s and 1970s, the show business community was becoming slightly more sensitive to

the roles given to Asian Americans, but more change was needed. Beulah and other concerned Asian actors founded the Association of Asian Pacific American Artists (AAPAA). The mission of AAPAA was to promote more realistic and balanced images of Asians in the media and to fight against stereotyping in television and movies. Beulah served as vice-president for several years and helped to lead AAPAA's fight. AAPAA members organized letter-writing campaigns and held direct discussions to educate Hollywood producers of their concerns.

Portraying the Features and Experiences of Asians

A major source of frustration and anger for Asian American actors on stage and in film was the portrayal of Asians by Caucasians in "Oriental" make-up. Examples are plentiful, from Rob Schneider as an Asian minister in *I Now Pronounce You Chuck and Larry* (2007) to actors Warner Oland, Sidney Toler, Roland Winters and Peter Ustinov playing Charlie Chan in a series of films between 1931-1981. Even well-known actors like John Wayne resorted to this crude technique when playing Genghis Khan in the 1956 film, *The Conqueror,* as did Tony Randall in *The 7 Faces of Dr. Lao* (1964). The "Oriental" make-up that white actors put on their faces was not a new thing; earlier, African Americans

---

12. Quoted in Crystal Chow, "*60 Years on the Silver Screen.*" *Rice*, Sept. 1988.

"Most of the time I would say they are not out to offend. It's just that they don't know. I have gone to producers several times and said, 'Look, you're going to get calls from the community on this — to say chink or Chinaman is not acceptable.' And those producers will be genuinely surprised."

— Beulah Kwoh

on stage and in theater were often portrayed by white actors in "blackface."

Beulah was an early pioneer in films in which Asian actors portrayed Asian characters. In the film *MacArthur* (1977), Beulah portrayed Ah Cheu while working with her acting friend, film legend Gregory Peck. Because of her association with East West Players, Beulah's stage involvement was also extensive. Beginning with her role in *Rashomon*, Beulah performed in many productions including *The Chinese Chess Piece* and East West Players' *Ikebana*, for which she earned a 1996 Dramalogue award for her outstanding theater performance.

In *The Children of An Lac*, a 1980 movie-of-the-week, Beulah played the role of Madame Ngai, the determined founder of an orphanage in war-torn Vietnam who saved hundreds of orphans in Saigon with the assistance of two American women. One of Beulah's memorable moments came in 1981 while working in China on NBC's *Marco Polo*. Beulah portrayed the empress of Kublai Khan in this major film project, the first of its kind allowed by the Chinese government to be made in China. During filming in the Forbidden City in Beijing, Beulah was carried in an ornate sedan chair by "a number of young men, all Chinese soldiers that had been selected to work in the film. I really enjoyed that!"[13]

13. Beulah Quo, Personal interview, 1995.

Reaching the American Public Through Television

Few people outside of the Asian American community had any familiarity with the long and complex history of Asians in America. *Paper Angels*, a 1985 American Playhouse TV production, was very significant, for it provided an opportunity for Asian American actors to participate in a quality production focusing on the Asian American experience. Beulah portrayed Chin Moo, an immigrant being held in the immigration station barracks on Angel Island, the San Francisco port of entry. Drawing upon her understanding of the experiences of some of her own relatives who passed through Angel Island, Beulah gave an intense performance that captured the determination, hope, and fears of these immigrants. In doing so she educated television viewers to the dehumanizing detention of thousands of Chinese immigrants in Angel Island.

Believing strongly in the power of the media to shape people's perceptions of Asian Americans, Beulah worked actively behind the camera as well. In the early 1970s, she became the first Asian American to produce a public affairs television program dealing with issues affecting the Asian American community. Aired by KNBC television, *Expressions: East-West* was moderated by her fellow Asian American actor and activist, George Takei. Most well-known for his role as Mr. Sulu on TV's *Star Trek*, George became a close and lifelong friend.

Beulah was also the first Asian American woman to earn a local Emmy when she created and produced the documentary *James Wong Howe: The Man and His Movies* for KNBC. Until then, few outside of Hollywood knew anything of this gifted and legendary cinematographer whose artistry behind the camera brought life to over 125 movie classics including *The Rose Tattoo*, *Hud*, and *Funny Girl*.

In 1998 Beulah was appointed to the Sesquicentennial Commission charged with the responsibility of organizing the celebration of California's 150 years of statehood. Members of the commission were chosen for their leadership roles throughout the state. Recognizing once again an opportunity to educate the public about the often-overlooked contributions of Asian Americans to the development of our country, Beulah commissioned and helped to raise funds for a musical about the struggles of the early Asian immigrants in California. The resulting piece, *Heading East*, was performed in several venues in California as part of the state sesquicentennial celebration. A traveling exhibition of photos documenting 100 years of Asian Pacific American history in California accompanied the musical as it toured throughout the state.

Seeking Justice on Stage

"With Beulah, no stone was left unturned. She rolled them with her own energy if they couldn't or wouldn't move on their own!"[14]

– George Takei, actor

Beulah's determination to develop awareness in the community at large about Asian American issues was channeled into several greatly significant projects during the 1980s and 1990s. The first began in 1982 in response to the tragic murder of Vincent Chin, a young Chinese American man who had lived in Detroit. Beaten to death by two displaced white autoworkers on the eve of his wedding, Chin had been mistaken by the angry and frustrated men to be Japanese. The two killers were subsequently only given parole for having committed this brutal, racially-motivated crime.

Beulah and Edwin invited Vincent's mother, Lily, to stay at their home when she visited Los Angeles to

Various roles: *from top,* Beulah Kwoh as Empress Chabi in NBC's *Marco Polo*, 1982. *Middle*: playing a grandmother in an episode of *Hawaii Five-O. Bottom*: Quo as Elvis Presley's adoptive mother in *Girls, Girls, Girls*, 1962.

PHOTOS COURTESY OF AUDREY MAGAZINE

14. George Takei, Telephone interview, April 4, 2005.

"With Beulah, no stone was left unturned. She rolled them with her own energy if they couldn't or wouldn't move on their own!"

— *George Takei*

speak at one of the many rallies that were being organized around the country in the wake of her son's murder. Beulah grew increasingly outraged over the unjust outcomes and became convinced that Vincent's story needed to be told, but from his mother's point of view. Lily Chin, too, was desperate to "do everything I can to make sure that no other mother goes through what I went through."[15] Lily had become an initially reluctant but increasingly influential and powerful activist. Trusting Beulah to help her in this cause, Lily Chin gave the story rights of Vincent's case to her.

Armed with her characteristic energy, creativity, and determination, Beulah contacted Yang Xie, a Chinese film director, and Cherylene Lee, a Chinese American playwright and former child actor whom she had known for many years. The two collaborated on a screenplay called *And Justice for All*. Then in 1997, Cherylene was asked by the director of the Contemporary American Theatre Festival to write a play based on the screenplay that she and Yang Xie had written.

Thanks in large part to the fundraising efforts of Beulah and Cherylene, the resulting play, *Carry the Tiger to the Mountain*, premiered on July 10, 1998 in Shepherdstown, West Virginia, with Beulah playing the lead role of Lily Chin, Vincent's courageous mother. "I think Beulah and I shook hands with every possible donor in West Virginia, Virginia, Baltimore, and Washington, D.C.!"[16] Through their efforts, the play and theater became a line item in the governor of West Virginia's budget and part of the governor's policy for his statewide Initiative on Race.

Carry the Tiger to the Mountain went on to be performed in New York at the Pan Asian Repertory Theatre and in Los Angeles at East West Players. There, Beulah recreated her role as Lily Chin, her moving, anguished performance a fitting tribute to the courageous mother who sought justice for her murdered son.

Exclusion Leads to Unity

In a favorite recollection that Beulah liked to share, she and some of her fellow actors, comprised of African Americans, Latinos, Asian Americans and other minorities, were on a sightseeing trip in Salt Lake City and went to visit the great Mormon

15. Quoted in Daniel Yi, "*Beulah and Stewart Quo*" A. Magazine: Inside Asian America, April 1996.
16. Cherylene Lee, E-mail to the author, June 7, 2005.

"Beulah was an actor in the true definition of the word — a person who takes action."[17]

— *George Takei*

Tabernacle. However, before they could set foot in the tabernacle, they were told that they could not enter. Though they found out later that it was because they were not of the Mormon faith, they initially joked amongst themselves. Had they been denied entry because of the African Americans? The Asian Americans? The Latinos among them? This early sense of exclusion left a lasting impression upon Beulah, for she and her friends found not only comfort in the shared experience, but feelings of unity and solidarity as well.

That Beulah believed strongly in the importance of bringing people of all colors together was reflected in her extensive service to the Los Angeles community. She served on the Los Angeles City Human Relations Committee, on the board of directors for United Way, El Nido Services (a family counseling agency) and many others. In recognition of her dedicated service, she earned a place in the California Public Education Hall of Fame. And in 1999, she was selected to be the 45th Assembly District's Woman of the Year by Los Angeles Mayor Antonio Villaraigosa who was then Speaker of the California State Assembly.

The fight to portray Asian Americans and other ethnic groups accurately and to open up opportunities for actors of color has continued since our mother's passing in 2002. Asian Americans are still underrepresented on TV and in movies.[18]

But compared to fifty years ago, significant progress has been made, in large part, due to the selfless work of our mother. Asian Americans are no longer the invisible, stereotyped characters of our childhood; they are emerging as multidimensional individuals — doctors, artists, detectives, parents, and children — all members of today's rich and colorful American landscape. Early in her long and illustrious career, our mother recognized the enormous potential to use the silver screen as more than a means of entertainment. In her tireless and courageous efforts to break down barriers and seek justice through the medium of film and stage, her dedicated service to the community, and her sensitive portrayals of a myriad of characters, our mother's heroic legacy lives on.

17. Quoted in Sara Ki, "The Many Splendored Facets of Beulah Quo." *Audrey*, March 2003.

18. National Asian Pacific American Legal Consortium, *Asian Pacific Americans in Prime Time: Lights, Camera, and Little Action*, 2005.

Photo: K.W. Lee in 1969, reporting on daily accounts of a West Virginia family's life on isolated Doctors Creek. Photo courtesy of K.W. Lee.

Building Bridges between Races:
Kyung Won Lee, Investigative Journalist

ANGELA OH

K.W. Lee is a Man Who Moves My Heart

My heart was moved from the very first time I heard him speaking out against injustice around the Chol Soo Lee case in the 1970s. Subsequently, I heard and read K.W. Lee speaking and writing about immigration and labor issues in the 1980s, and, in 1992, about the Los Angeles Rebellion, that unfairly pitted minorities against one another.

I think that K.W. Lee has always been a man who breaks barriers and builds bridges: between African Americans, Latinos, and Asian Americans, between rich and poor, between those inside and outside of prisons, and between generations — those born in America and those from other lands. In fact, K.W. thinks of *our* futures — together. It is K.W. Lee's capacity to extend himself beyond his individual soul and profession, and to reach out to others in diverse communities, that distinguishes him — maverick, award-winning investigative journalist — from so many others. From the 1950s when he first immigrated to the U.S., K.W. has been a pathbreaking journalist, reporter, and editor.

In K.W. Lee's view, the Korean American community is at the threshold of a new era in which "a community conscience" is forming. These Korean Americans, many of them a younger generation, find themselves working in labor struggles for both Asians and Latinos, of becoming part of multicultural civil rights organizations, or involved in community non-profit agencies to improve the lives of all people within the Los Angeles community.

K.W. Lee believes in this multiracial, pluralistic future. And this is the foundation of the hope he continues to express — the hope he will never let die.

A Journalist's Journey toward Justice

In 1950, at the age of 21, K.W. Lee arrived in the United States, having studied English literature while at Korea University. Like so many students who arrived in America after the Korean war, K.W. Lee believed he would finish his studies and return to Korea to help run an English newspaper in the post Korean war era, building on the strong sense of cultural nationalism he felt. His dreams of returning to Korea never materialized. Instead, he found himself in the midst of another struggle in the heart of the United States — the 1960s Civil Rights Movement.

Breaking Color Barriers — before the Civil Rights Movement

As a young reporter employed in the South a decade before the start of the 1960s Civil Rights Movement, K.W. Lee had the chance to confront the color-line in local news reporting. He wrote about four young African American high school graduates who dared to ask to be acknowledged in connection with their scholastic achievements in the local newspaper in the southern town of Kingsport, Tennessee.

Koreans in the U.S.

The United States is a nation of immigrants. One of latest and fastest growing ethnic communities in the United States is that of the Korean Americans. The Korean immigrant experience in the U.S. can be traced back one hundred years but it is only since 1965 that the numbers have been substantial.

From the very beginnings of the United States anti-Asian attitudes were present. The Act of 1790 prevented Asian immigrants from becoming naturalized citizens. The Nationality Origins Act in 1924 declared all persons born of Asian ancestry were barred to immigrate because they were ruled ineligible to become American citizens. In 1952 the passage of the McCarran-Walter Immigration Act allowed Korea and Japan each an annual quota of 100 people who could immigrate to America. The law also allowed alien residents of Korean ancestry in America the right for naturalization, thus ending the discriminatory law of naturalization based on race and ethnic origin.

In 1965, the Immigration Act abolished the quota system that had restricted the numbers of Asians allowed to enter the United States. Large numbers of Koreans, including some from the North that have come via South Korea, have been immigrating ever since, putting Korea in the top five countries of origin of immigrants to the United States since 1975. The reasons for immigration include the desire for increased freedom, especially for women, and the hope for better economic opportunities.

Later, in Appalachia, he challenged those who sought profit, trading on the lives of working people and their families, by illuminating the problem of black lung disease among coal miners of Appalachia.

As a cub reporter at the crusading *Charleston Gazette* in West Virginia, K.W. Lee was assigned to cover the marches and protests that were organized in the Appalachian south by African Americans seeking to end racial discrimination. He recalls "In Appalachia I saw poverty, despair and corruption eyeball to eyeball. Disenfranchised mountain folk — both black and white — grew on me. I was assigned to be out in the trenches to open up Jim Crow places — hotels, restaurants and cafes. I was so involved in this thing I didn't realize until much later that I was courting danger at a time when the old world was on its last stand against the coming new eras."

"Why was that man wearing a mask?"

Carole Ferrell, who worked for the West Virginia Commission on Human Rights for twenty years, remembers K.W. Lee well:

K.W. was the first American of Asian descent I'd ever met. I was reared in a Southern West Virginia coal mining community, went to segregated schools, and was educated at a historically black college — the occasion to have a relationship with an Asian American in West Virginia was almost nil. I became very conscious of how little my children knew about Asians when my oldest son — then five — met K.W. at my office. Later, my son asked, "Mother, why was that man wearing a mask?"

The "mask" would prove to be the single most important thing that K.W. Lee would dedicate his life to removing. As events would unfold in later years, K.W.

Photos, top: K.W. Lee standing in front yard of one of the two West Virginia families on isolated Doctors Creek with whom he spent days for daily accounts of their life in 1969, with children playing in the background.

Right, K.W. Lee with children of the Bresindine and Zornes families, on front porch of the Bresindine house, with Mrs. Myrtle Zornes partially hidden in the back.

*Photo: K.W. Lee's first 1977 interview with inmate Chol Soo Lee at Deuel
State Prison near Stockton, California.*

> *K.W. Lee believes in this multi-
> racial, pluralistic future. And
> this is the foundation of the hope
> he continues to express — the
> hope he will never let die.*
>
> — *Angela Oh*

Lee found that the task of removing the stereotypes,
the ignorance, and the bigotry against Korean Americans and Asian Americans was formidable.

When he moved to the West Coast of the United
States, he continued his crusade in journalism.

How a Journalist Helped Free Imprisoned Youth

K.W. Lee was the primary reporter who wrote
about the Chol Soo Lee case, and spearheaded
a pan-Asian movement to free this youth who
was unjustly imprisoned for life.

In 1977, K.W. Lee met a prison inmate named
Chol Soo Lee. The young Korean immigrant was
charged with first-degree murder for stabbing to
death another inmate, a reputed neo-Nazi, in a prison
yard altercation at Deuel State Prison in Tracy, California. Lee claimed self-defense. At the time of the
prison incident, Chol Soo was already serving time

for the murder of reputed gang adviser Yip Yee Tak in San Francisco's Chinatown. The prison killing was prosecuted as a death penalty case with special circumstances under California law due to the fact that Chol Soo was already serving a life-term for murder.

Upon learning of Chol Soo's case, K.W. Lee, then working for the *Sacramento Union*, felt a strong urge to take a closer look — the story did not seem to add up. He wanted to learn more about the case by going straight to the source. He interviewed Chol Soo, obtained authorization to review files, and in so doing, K.W. Lee was convinced that the young Korean immigrant was wrongfully convicted. Thus began the crusade to do everything that could possibly be done to save an innocent man.

With the help of a handful of committed young lawyers and community members, K.W. Lee mounted a national campaign that sparked Korean Americans and others to save the life of Chol Soo Lee. This core team of supporters sought K.W. Lee's help in the case when the prison murder case broke.

The challenge of working across ethnic community lines was enormous. The infrastructure had to be built from the ground up.

The first victory in the campaign came when a Sacramento Superior Court judge granted Chol Soo Lee's request for a new trial in 1979. Then, in 1982, in the retrial of the Chinatown case, a San Francisco jury acquitted Chol Soo Lee of the first murder conviction, and his prison murder conviction was nullified on appeal. Then, in 1983, Chol Soo was finally free, after spending ten years in prison (eight of those years in solitary confinement and four of those years on death row).

Utilizing Media to Build a Community: *Koreatown Weekly*

In 1979, K.W. Lee took on the role of editor-publisher of the English-language newspaper, *Koreatown Weekly*. It was an opportunity to meet and mentor young Korean American journalists, many of whom view K.W. Lee as the icon of their profession. But K.W. Lee did not limit opportunities at his weekly to Korean Americans; rather, he encouraged writers of other ethnic backgrounds to explore newly unfolding developments that *Koreatown Weekly* covered.

For four years, until 1982, this newspaper focused on creating a media to serve a new, emerging multiethnic and bilingual society. K.W. Lee foresaw the importance of reaching out to the emerging 1.5 Korean generation (those born in Korea but raised in America) and a growing U.S.–born 2.0, or second, generation.

The L.A. Rebellion/Riots, May 1992 Challenges a Reporter

Background

In 1991, the beating of Rodney King, an African American, by four LAPD officers was caught on video. The officers went on trial and on April 29, 1992, twelve jurors in Sylmar, California, delivered their verdicts in the controversial case. The case had received heavy media coverage when a video of the beating hit the national airwaves. The verdicts came as a complete surprise: One of the officers was found guilty of excessive force; the other officers were cleared of all charges.

The "mask" would prove to be the single most important thing that K.W. Lee would dedicate his life to removing. As events would unfold in later years, K.W. found that the task of removing the stereotypes, the ignorance, and the bigotry against Korean Americans and Asian Americans was formidable.

— Angela Oh

The verdicts were broadcast live, and anger spread throughout the city. For three days the city experienced widespread devastation. Approximately 3,600 fires were set, destroying 1,100 buildings. This proved to be the most destructive civil unrest since 1965. The final tally:

- More than 50 killed
- Over 4,000 injured, 12,000 people arrested
- $1 billion in property damage (Korean American businesses lost $425 million of that amount).

K.W. Lee called the L.A. Rebellion of 1992 "America's first media-fanned urban mob assault on a hapless tribe of newcomers with no voice or clout." The spring of 1992, commonly known as the L.A. Rebellion or L.A. Riots was a season of tragedy for African Americans, Latinos, Korean Americans, and others living in Los Angeles. Koreans across the globe were shaken when the looting, vandalism, and arson left more than 2,500 immigrant families stripped down to nothing.

Recognizing K.W.'s Contributions

The 1990s was a period of high unemployment, poor police/community relations, no investment in the city's infrastructure, and major high profile cases involving African American victims of crime and non-African American defendants.

K.W. Lee sensed an escalating tension in South Central Los Angeles. He quickly recruited a young, multi-ethnic staff, mostly fresh out of college, and launched the *Korea Times* English-language weekly in 1990. By 1992, K.W. Lee was in the hospital, his health had been failing him and his liver reached its end stage of deterioration due to the hepatitis B virus. As he waited for a new liver, Los Angeles imploded. The fuse — the verdict in the Rodney King trial.

K.W. Lee's efforts during this critical period was recognized by Los Angeles County. In 1992, he was among 13 individuals honored by the L.A. County Human Relations Commission. He was recognized for "promoting intergroup relations, through journalism and through community involvement, using genuine portrayals of real people to foster genuine understanding." The following is K.W. Lee's speech in accepting the award:

> *K.W. Lee called the L.A. Rebellion of 1992 "America's first media-fanned urban mob assault on a hapless tribe of newcomers with no voice or clout."*
> — *Angela Oh*

Understanding Word Connotation

The 1992 upheaval in Los Angeles is described by several terms: LA Riots, LA Rebellion, LA Uprising.

What does the selection of one term over another reveal?

"*S*ix months have elapsed, since the four days of fire, fury and madness. We Korean Americans in the Southland still remain stunned, bewildered, confused, abandoned and terribly lost.

Few ethnic minorities have been so devastated with such a blow since World War II, singled out for destruction as the newest scapegoat for all the ills — imagined or real — of the murderous inner cities of our country.

It's been the year of our economic Holocaust. Almost every member of my people, nearly a quarter million immigrants in the Southland, have been decimated by this madness and calamity. It's as if we have committed an unpardonable crime of being born Korean. We look up to heaven and ask, "Why us, why Korean American, why Koreatown?"

The history of newcomers from Korea is as young, fledgling and innocent as 15-year-old Latasha Harlins, but it is literally being written in blood, tears and sweat.

Each day, a new chapter unfolds.

And my small newspaper is here to chronicle their struggle, telling the untold story of our people — with warts and all — in their full human context, not only for the outsiders, but for our future generations.

The impact of the local media's race mongering has been instantaneous and devastating when it comes to our relationship with our black brothers and sisters, especially in South Central. Even before they had a chance to know each other — who they are, where they've been and their common struggle of the past — both Korean Americans and African Americans were pitted against each other in the local media as enemies in the shouting sound bites and the screaming headlines.

And our newspaper has been trying our damnedest to undo the accumulated neglects and wrongs of the past years, but it's like a cry in the wilderness, a whisper in the wind.

Internally, our paper is also developing an ongoing dialogue among the diverse and disparate elements of my subterranean community — between children and their parents, the Korean-born and the American-born, the newcomers, the latecomers and the early comers.

But the Korean-speaking parents and the English-speaking children seem to march to their own drums. It's like two ships passing each other in a dark night without even exchanging a signal. This is our particular sorrow.

PHOTOS COURTESY OF K.W. LEE

Photos, from above: K.W. Lee reunited in 2000 in Charleston with the Rev. Homer Davis, who led sustained civil rights struggles in West Virginia in the 1960s in alliance with the Southern Christian Leadership Conference.

Middle: reunited with civil rights activist Carole Ferrell in front of the California state capitol in 2000.

Bottom: K.W. and his Korea Times Weekly staff reporters in a get together with Los Angeles Sentinel staffers in South Central L.A. in 1991, a year prior to the L.A. Riots, as part of the "Good Neighbor Exchange" program.

> *"Again, when it comes to relations with our ethnic brothers and sisters, we try to adhere to the highest standards of accuracy, fairness and balanced reporting. Every copy is being scrutinized because we know lives and limbs and livelihoods are at stake."*
> — K.W. Lee

Above all, my paper is committed to serving as a bridge to our ethnic brothers and sisters. And we have run hundreds of stories about Korean merchants trying to live as good neighbors in the non-Korean neighborhoods.

We have also taken the initiative of having exchanges with such respected newspapers as the Los Angeles Sentinel, Jewish Journal, Rafu Shimpo and others. We have visited our counterparts in South Central to get to know them. Their columns and editorials grace our newspaper most regularly.

PHOTOS ON THIS PAGE ©1992 HYUNGWON KANG/LOS ANGELES TIMES

Photos: top, Korean-owned shops burn during the 1992 Los Angeles Riots in Koreatown, April 30, 1992. Right, hundreds rally for peace in Koreatown.

Photo: K.W. addressing the huge crowd that packed Seoul International Park in the heart of Koreatown during the 10th anniversary rally of the 1992 Los Angeles Riots.

"My new liver may have belonged to an African American or a Latino or an Anglo. What does it matter? We are all entangled in an unbroken human chain of interdependence and mutual survival."

— *K.W. Lee*

Again, when it comes to relations with our ethnic brothers and sisters, we try to adhere to the highest standards of accuracy, fairness and balanced reporting. Every copy is being scrutinized because we know the lives and limbs and livelihoods are at stake.

May 2nd, the day after the three days of burning and looting, was our finest moment.

While the buildings along the streets were still smoldering, a sea of more than 30,000 Korean Americans, young and old with their children, held the largest Asian American demonstration of peace in this nation's history.

Young and old alike, with (Anglo) African American and Latino supporters, marched while chanting for peace and racial harmony.

It was our glorious Martin Luther King Day. And we shall overcome hatred and fear, the mother of all violence. It was the day the torch also was passed to our American-born, English-speaking children, our second generation.

And the Korean Americans are no longer here as sojourners or guests. We are here to live and die in the urban trenches because we have given so much of ourselves and gained so much in freedom in return.

This is our last home on this Earth.

On a final and very personal note, may I add that I believe in the resurrection of the City of Angels.

You are looking at a living and breathing example of the magic miracles performed quietly in this so-called never-never land of murder, mayhem and madness. I am recovering from a recent liver transplant operation at the UCLA Medical Center, where hundreds of health care people of all colors are bound together to save fragile human lives from the terminal diseases with transplants.

My new liver may have belonged to an African American or a Latino or an Anglo. What does it matter? We are all entangled in an unbroken human chain of interdependence and mutual survival.

And what really matters is that we all belong to each other during our earthly passage."

Chapter 4

Fighting for Constitutional Rights
During and after World War II

"Are we Americans or not? Are we citizens of this country? They can put us away without a hearing. If you look like the enemy they can put you in a box."

–Fred Korematsu

"It is less painful to remember the atrocities and brutalities of the war than to think of the denial of our military service in the U.S. Armed Forces."

–Manong Faustino "Peping" Baclig

*Photo: Fred Korematsu holding a letter from the U.S Government apologizing
for its unjust internment of Japanese Americans during World War II.*

One Man Seeks Justice from a Nation: *Korematsu v. United States*

ERIC YAMAMOTO, DALE MINAMI AND MAY LEE HEYE

"Mr. Korematsu, I just want to tell you that I saw you speak to my class two years ago at UC Berkeley, and you are the reason that I went to law school."

–Josephine Yeh
First year law student
March 1999

Today, in law classes throughout the nation, *Korematsu v. United States* is studied as a central case of American constitutional law. Fred Korematsu challenged the United States two times: the first time in 1944, in which he defied the U.S. government's unconstitutional internment of Japanese Americans and refused to go into the camps, and the second time in 1983, in which his original 1944 conviction for refusing to go into the concentration camps was overturned by the federal court in San Francisco.

After September 11, 2001, Arabs, Middle Easterners, and South Asians in the U.S. often found themselves the victims of racial and media profiling and societal violence.

Some individuals were detained and incarcerated in prisons within the U.S. or placed in internment camps abroad, including Guantanamo Bay in Cuba. These groups are re-examining the Korematsu case in relation to asserting and vindicating their own legal, civil, and constitutional rights.

Born in the U.S.A.

Born in 1919, Fred Toyosaburo Korematsu grew up in Oakland as one of four sons of Japanese immigrants. His family owned a rose nursery, and he attended Castlemont High School, where his closest friends and girlfriend were Caucasian. "Being born in this country, I learned about American history, and this was my country," he remembers, "I just thought of myself as American." After graduation from high school in 1938, he attended the Master School of Welding and went to work on the Oakland docks as a steel welder, where he was quickly promoted to a foreman position.

The war in Europe, however, changed his life. America began providing war supplies to Great Britain in their war against Germany, while German allies — the Japanese — waged war in Asia and the Pacific. At home in California, when Fred entered restaurants, waiters refused to serve him. The same thing happened when he tried to get his hair cut. When he tried to join the United States Coast Guard along with his Caucasian friends, he was not allowed to fill out an application. "We have orders not to accept you," he was told by the recruiting officer. Later, a commanding officer even forbade one of his friends from associating with him. The Boiler Makers Union terminated his membership. He eventually found work with a trailer mobile company, but after the Japanese bombing of Pearl Harbor in December 1941, his employer fired him.

What Happened to Japanese Americans in 1942

On February 19, 1942, President Roosevelt signed Executive Order 9066 authorizing the military commanders on the West Coast to issue whatever orders were necessary for national security, including the removal of 120,000 Japanese Americans from the West Coast. Curfew and exclusionary orders soon followed. Japanese Americans were placed in remote desert and mountain concentration camps in barracks, guarded by barbed wire and guntowers.

Although his family reported to the Tanforan racetrack assembly center in San Mateo on May 9, 1942, as directed by Exclusion Order Number 34, twenty-two-year-old Fred chose to defy the order.

With his Caucasian girlfriend, Fred planned to move inland to Nevada. He sold his car, threw away his California driver's license, and on his draft card

Photos: this page, Fred Korematsu as a child inside the family's rose nursery. Opposite page, Fred and family, circa 1939.

assumed a new identity as Clyde Sarah, a Las Vegas-born Spanish Hawaiian. Fred even had plastic surgery in an attempt to change his appearance. Nevertheless, the police stopped him on May 30, 1942 in San Leandro, California and turned him over to the FBI. He was charged with violating the military's exclusion order. A newspaper headline read, "*Jap Spy Arrested in San Leandro.*"

While in the San Francisco federal prison, the Executive Director of the American Civil Liberties Union of Northern California, Ernest Besig, read about Fred's situation in the newspaper and offered to defend him. After spending two and a half months in jail, Fred was released when Besig paid his $5,000 bail. The moment they stepped outside of the courthouse into the sunshine, however, military authorities handcuffed him and took him to the Tanforan Assembly Center.

Tanforan Assembly Center was a racetrack that had been hastily converted to hold thousands of Japanese-American families. Armed guards manned watchtowers. Barbed wire surrounded the entire area. At night, searchlights swept the camp watching for anyone attempting to escape. Like the other internees, Fred lived in a horse stall. "The stall had one big door to let the horse in and there was an opening of six to eight inches at the bottom where the wind was blowing right through. It was a dirt floor, with straw on top of a cot, and a light up above; that was it. That was your room."

How Korematsu Challenged the Exclusion Order

Although imprisoned at Tanforan, Fred chose to challenge the exclusion order instead of pleading guilty. "The internment was wrong," he reasoned, "we didn't do anything disloyal." Nonetheless, he had little support from within the Japanese American community. The Japanese American Citizens League (JACL, a civil rights organization, founded in 1929) initially did not support his constitutional challenge.

Other Japanese Americans knew about him and avoided him, fearing for the safety of their own families. The federal district court in San Francisco ultimately found Fred guilty of violating military exclusion orders and sentenced him to five years probation under military authority. Attorneys from the ACLU appealed.

Upon his "release" on probation by criminal authorities, Fred was incarcerated in what he calls the "concentration camp." Fred and his family were moved to Topaz, Utah. After a year-and-a-half of laboring in the internment camp, Fred's qualifications as a skilled welder enabled him to leave the camp, provided that he not return to California. He got a

PHOTOS COURTESY OF KAREN KOREMATSU

"Being born in this country, I learned about American history, and this was my country . . . I just thought of myself as American."

— *Fred Korematsu*

"The stall had one big door to let the horse in and there was an opening of six to eight inches at the bottom where the wind was blowing right through. It was a dirt floor, with straw on top of a cot, and a light up above; that was it. That was your room."

— Fred Korematsu

Hirabayashi and Yasui

In addition to Fred Korematsu, two other young Japanese Americans, Minoru "Min" Yasui and Gordon Hirabayashi, defied the government's policies against Japanese Americans. Public Proclamation No. 3 issued by General John L. DeWitt, Military Commander of the Western Defense Command, imposed travel restrictions and a curfew on German, Italian, and Japanese nationals. However, it was also used against Americans of Japanese ancestry. The curfew required Japanese Americans to be indoors between 8 p.m. to 6 a.m.

Living in different cities and acting alone, Min and Gordon tested the constitutionality of the government's actions.

Minoru "Min" Yasui, a young lawyer, challenged the constitutionality of the curfew order. He began walking the streets of Portland, Oregon after 8 p.m. deliberately breaking the curfew. He approached a police officer and explained he was breaking curfew and asked to be arrested. The police officer told him to go home. He then walked into a police station, and an officer there accommodated his request.

Gordon Hirabayashi was a senior at the University of Washington. To comply with curfew, Gordon had to rush back to his dorm room while other students continued their own routines. He became angry. He was an American citizen and had done nothing wrong, so he decided to ignore the curfew order. No one at the university turned him in. When ordered to evacuate, Gordon openly defied the order.

Both Yasui and Hirabayashi were arrested, tried and convicted for their defiance. Like Fred Korematsu, their cases were appealed to the Supreme Court and like Korematsu, the Supreme Court upheld their convictions.

Many years later, Min and Gordon returned to the courts and were vindicated when their convictions were vacated. (Vacated is the legal term that means a conviction is dismissed.)

job as a welder in an iron works company in Salt Lake City. Eventually he made his way to Detroit.

The Supreme Court Case, 1944

Fred's appeal eventually reached the Supreme Court in 1944. The Court upheld the lower court's ruling in a 6-3 vote, sadly holding the U.S. Congressional and military rationalizations for interning Japanese Americans based on possible "disloyal members" who might have "constituted a menace to the national defense and safety."

And, in a statement that speaks volumes of the absurdity of this decision, the court declared, "Korematsu was not excluded from the Military Area because of hostility to him or his race."

Fred petitioned for a rehearing, but it was denied in February 1945. He was devastated. He had lost; Japanese Americans had lost; the Constitution had failed him. He worried about the impact his ruling may have on his own children and other Japanese Americans. "Are we Americans or not? Are we citizens of this country? They can put us away without a hearing. If you look like the enemy they can put you in a box."

Korematsu Challenges the Court Again, 1983

Fred hoped to reopen his case someday. He did not know, however, how he could do so, or who would help. The long road to the reconsideration of the Korematsu, Yasui, and Hirabayashi internment cases began with a letter from history professor Peter Irons. Irons and Aiko Herzig-Yoshinaga had discovered irrefutable evidence that top government officials knew and covered up significant government intelligence information that the Japanese Americans had not actually posed a threat to national security at the time of the internment. That evidence also revealed that top U.S. Justice Department officials, including the Solicitor General, lied to the Supreme Court about the "military necessity" justification for the internment. As the evidence of government misconduct began to accumulate, the possibility of reopening his case became more of a reality.

Three legal teams in San Francisco, Seattle, and Portland representing Korematsu, Hirabayashi and Yasui, respectively, made this unprecedented attempt to overturn cases that had been earlier decided by the Supreme Court.

Photo: Korematsu Legal Team at "60 Minutes" interview in 1983, from left to right: Donald Tamaki, Dale Minami, Karen Kai, Dennis Hayashi.

On January 19, 1983, a volunteer legal team filed a petition for writ of error *coram nobis* at the San Francisco federal district court for Fred Korematsu. This type of legal proceeding is so little known that the clerk had to ask whether they wanted it filed as a civil or criminal suit. A writ of *coram nobis* is limited to rare cases in which the courts are compelled to correct "fundamental error," or "manifest injustice" in their own processes, which are discovered after a person has been convicted and released from prison.

Young Lawyers Challenge Injustice

Many of the lawyers, clerks and student volunteers were third-generation Japanese Americans whose parents and grandparents had been incarcerated. "When they first showed up at my house, I thought they looked like high school kids," Mr. Korematsu recalls. The team of pro bono attorneys committed themselves to high intensity lawyering for eighteen months not only to clear Korematsu, Hirabayashi and Yasui, but also to vindicate all Japanese American internees.

They did so with three purposes in mind: first, to educate the American public by correcting the historical record that branded Japanese Americans as disloyal during World War II; second, to attack the precedent created through the three earlier Supreme Court cases that upheld the imprisonment of an entire minority group without charges, hearings or attorneys; and, third, to overturn the convictions of these three courageous men who stood up, virtually alone, to challenge the government's racially discriminatory actions.

Despite the compelling evidence produced, the legal team still faced a monumental task — to reconstruct events 40 years before which denied a fair hearing.

Korematsu's Second Day in Court

At one point in the litigation, for instance, Fred was offered a pardon by the government. He rejected this offer, telling the legal team, "I don't want a pardon. If anything, I should be pardoning the government." So on that drizzly fall day in November, 1983, in a packed ceremonial federal courtroom, Dale Minami, Fred's lead counsel, argued that the public interest demanded nullification of his conviction. Nullification of this individual's conviction would also expose the injustice of the massive incarceration of other Japanese Americans.

Minami stated:

> This is not just a 40-year-old misdemeanor, as the government characterizes it. This is a monumental precedent which affected deeply and irrevocably the lives of 120,000 Japanese Americans, and countless numbers of friends and neighbors by the mass banishment of a single racial minority group . . . The public interest, then, demands more than a sterile recitation that we should let bygones be bygones and requires that the real substantial reasons [for the imprisonment] be exposed so that this tragedy will never be repeated.

"The internment was wrong. We didn't do anything disloyal."

— Fred Korematsu

Victor Stone, the United States Attorney representing the government, argued against such a position. The Court was silent and still when Fred stood to address the court that had convicted him 41 years earlier. In a simple but powerful manner he said:

> As an American citizen being put through this shame and embarrassment and also all Japanese American citizens who were escorted to concentration camps, suffered the same embarrassment, we can never forget this incident as long as we live . . . As long as my record stands in federal court, any American citizen can be held in prison or concentration camps without a trial or a hearing . . . Therefore, I would like to see the government admit that they were wrong and do something about it so this will never happen again to any American citizen of any race, creed or color.

At the conclusion of argument, United States District Court Judge Marilyn Patel ruled from the bench, vacating Mr. Korematsu's conviction on grounds of "manifest injustice." In her ruling, Judge Patel found that

> [The] records show the facts upon which the military necessity justification for the Executive Order, namely Executive Order 9066, the legislative act . . . and the exclusion orders . . . were based upon and relied upon by the government in its arguments to the Court and to the Supreme Court on unsubstantiated facts, distortions and representations of at least one

PHOTO COURTESY OF KAREN KOREMATSU

Photo: Dale Minami, Fred Korematsu, Ernest Besig.

Photo: Fred Korematsu and Rosa Parks at ACLU of Northern California Bill of Rights Day.

military commander, whose views were seriously in-fected by racism.

She went on to comment on the claims of military necessity by the government: The overwhelming number of Japanese were citizens, were residents of the United States, were loyal to the United States; that the various acts that suggested either the potential for espionage or sabotage that had occurred or could occur in the future, were essentially non-existent or were contradicted by evidence that was in the possession of the Navy, the Justice Department, the Federal Communications Commission and the Federal Bureau of Investigation.

In conclusion, Judge Patel commented on the lessons of *Korematsu v. United States*:

Korematsu remains on the pages of our legal and political history. As a legal precedent, it is now recognized as having very limited application. As historical precedent, it stands as a constant caution that in times of war or declared military necessity our institutions must be vigilant in protecting constitutional guaran-tees. It stands as a caution that in times of distress the shield of military necessity and national security must not be used to protect governmental actions from close scrutiny and accountability. It stands as a caution that in times of international hostility and antagonisms our institutions, legislative, executive and judicial, must be prepared to exercise their authority to protect all citizens from the petty fears and prejudices that are so easily aroused.

After Fred's conviction was overturned, federal district courts in Portland and Seattle also vacated Min Yasui's and Gordon Hirabayashi's convictions respectively, although Hirabayashi had to endure a full trial and further appeal to the Ninth Circuit before his convictions were erased.

Aftermath: Redress and Coram Nobis

The new rulings on the three main World War II internment cases armed the proponents of the internee redress movement with powerful arguments against the legal claims that what was done to Japanese Americans was constitutional as held by the Supreme Court during World War II. The *coram nobis* rulings also became widely publicized, undermining the widely held view that Japanese Americans were disloyal. In 1988, after intense community organizing and political lobbying, the 100th Congress passed the Civil Liberties Act, authorizing reparations and mandating a national apology. The apology, sent to each internee in a letter from Presidents Ronald Reagan and George H.W. Bush, read:

> *More than fifty years ago, the United States Government unjustly interned, evacuated, relocated or otherwise deprived you and many other Japanese Americans of your liberty. Today, on behalf of your fellow Americans, I offer my sincere apologies for the actions that unfairly denied Japanese Americans and their families fundamental liberties during World War II.*
>
> *In passing the Civil Liberties Act of 1988, we acknowledged the wrongs of the past and offered redress to those who endured such grave injustice. In retrospect, we understand that the nation's actions were rooted deeply in racial prejudice and wartime hysteria. We must learn from the past and dedicate ourselves as a nation to renewing the spirit of equality and our love of freedom. Working together, we can make the most of our great diversity.*
>
> *You and your family have my best wishes for the future.*

Fred's lead *coram nobis* counsel, Dale Minami, sounds a cautionary note, however. "I think the jury's out on the legacy of redress. Unless we continue the legacy of that struggle for other groups — like Latin American Japanese Americans and other minority groups — the legacy will have been wasted." Fred, speaking to young Asian Americans like Josephine Yeh, offers a similar warning.

Racial Profiling: Could it Happen Again?

"I hope this could never happen again. But it could and some [people] still think that what the government did was right. They don't understand what happened . . . Even though it was unconstitutional; you still have to tell them. You have to stay on your toes and be strong. That's what I want all of you kids to do. Be strong and do what you're doing, you're doing all right."

So is Fred correct? Could the internment, or something like it happen again? Could the United

"Are we Americans or not? Are we citizens of this country? They can put us away without a hearing. If you look like the enemy they can put you in a box."

— Fred Korematsu

PHOTO COURTESY OF SHIRLEY NAKAO

Photo: Fred Korematsu wearing the Presidential Medal of Freedom

PHOTO COURTESY OF KAREN KOREMATSU

". . . some [people] still think that what the government did was right. They don't under-stand what happened . . . Even though it was unconstitutional; you still have to tell them. You have to stay on your toes and be strong. That's what I want all of you kids to do. Be strong and do what you're doing, you're doing all right."

— Fred Korematsu

States government deprive American citizens of their fundamental rights falsely in the name of national se-curity solely by reason of those citizens' race or col-or or country of origin? "Any group that's different, unpopular, and less powerful is susceptible to being rolled over by the majority," asserts Donald K. Tama-ki, who helped reopen Mr. Korematsu's case in 1983.

Consider the 1944 *Korematsu v. United States* case — the decision that initially upheld the consti-tutionality of the Japanese American internment. The Supreme Court refused then to consider the issue be-fore them as a case of unjust racial discrimination. In-stead, the Court upheld the exclusion order reasoning that "[t]o cast [the] case into outlines of racial preju-dice, without reference to the real military dangers which were presented, merely confuse[d] the issue."

And consider the government's and public's over-heated, vilifying reactions to recent unsubstantiated charges of nuclear secrets spying for China by Chi-nese Americans. Could something similar to intern-ment happen again — or more specifically, given the presence of sufficient "national security" dan-gers, could the United States government again jus-tify the internment of American citizens based upon their ethnic background? A *Nightline* story recently aired echoing the same thoughts Fred expressed fifty years ago. The episode, titled *"What Happens When a Neighbor Looks Like an Enemy,"* chillingly revealed

the continuing inability of many Americans to grasp the distinction between American citizens of Asian ancestry and foreigners from Asian nations.

And after the September 11 attacks on New York and Washington D.C., the United States engaged in extensive racial and religious profiling and detention of Arabs, Middle Easterners, South Asians and Mus-lims in America, many of whom were citizens. The president claimed vast "national security" power over Americans without oversight by the courts. A civil rights official even predicted that if there were another attack the government would yield to public demands for the mass internment of Arab Americans.

But Fred Korematsu and other civil liberties ad-vocates fought back. Korematsu spoke out publicly and submitted a "friend of the court" legal brief to the U.S. Supreme Court in the Guantanamo Bay in-definite detention case. He reminded the country that grave harms to innocent people and to the na-tion itself result from mass racial incarceration dur-ing times of public fear. He asked us all to be vigilant — not only over outside threats to our safety, but also over government abuses of power that threaten our fundamental liberties.

So perhaps the question is not "could internment, or something like it, happen again," but rather, what will it take on all our parts to prevent it?

American Veteran in Exile: Manong Faustino "Peping" Baclig

CASIMIRO URBANO TOLENTINO

"I urge all Americans to recall the courage, sacrifices and loyalty of Filipino veterans of World War II and honor them for their contribution to our freedom."

–President William J. Clinton on a Proclamation declaring October 20, 1996 as a day honoring Filipino veterans of WWII.

How I Know Manong "Peping" Baclig

For many of my generation growing up in the 1960s and 1970s, we did not have Filipino heroes to model our actions. Philip Vera Cruz, a labor union leader, was one of these heroes, whom I met and taught about when I was studying at UCLA. Faustino "Peping" Baclig has been added to that short list of heroes. Throughout this chapter I will refer to "Peping" with the Filipino term of *Manong*, a sign of respect, meaning "older brother" not necessarily a relative.

Manong Faustino "Peping" Baclig, as a Filipino soldier, fought alongside American soldiers during World War II and survived the infamous Bataan Death March.

During the past 60 years, he has led the struggle to claim benefits for Filipino American veterans. In doing so, he has brought honor and dignity not only to his fellow veterans but to both the Filipino and Filipino American communities.

I first met Manong Peping at a conference at the University of Southern California (USC) convened by the Asian Pacific American Legal Center in the late 1980s to educate and rally the Los Angeles County Filipino American community about veterans' issues. At that time, I had been researching the issue of the lack of veterans benefits for certain Filipino veterans. My father, Lucio Tolentino, also a Bataan Death March veteran, was one of the lucky ones who was able to transition from the Philippine Scouts to the U.S. Army with its attendant benefits. My godfather (*Ninong*), Franco Arcebal, who served with my father, was not so lucky and was in attendance at the conference. Ninong Franco introduced me to Manong Peping as his comrade and spokesperson for the equity issue.

Historical Background

At the beginning of WWII, the Philippines were under United States control. The Philippines became a U.S. territory in 1898. In 1934, Congress passed the Tydings-McDuffie Act or the Philippine Independence Act. It provided that after a transitional period of 10 years, the Philippines would become independent.

On Nov. 15, 1935, the U.S. organized the Commonwealth of the Philippines, a transitional government that was to end on July 4, 1946. During this period, the Commonwealth government organized a Filipino army that was funded by the U.S. government.

Manong Peping, dressed and standing ramrod straight in Army khaki, spoke about the issue in passionate terms and the need to remember the personal sacrifices of Filipinos for freedom in the Pacific. A few years later, Manong Peping would chain himself to General MacArthur's statue at Los Angeles' MacArthur Park — in the same uniform.

A recent report in the *Los Angeles Times* explained the basis for the decades long struggle of the Filipino veterans:

"A 1942 legal opinion by the Veterans Administration determined that the soldiers were eligible for benefits on the same basis as U.S. veterans. But many saw that decision as disproportionately benefiting Filipinos because of the lower cost of living in the Philippines. In 1946, Congress decided those soldiers would 'not be deemed to be or to have been' in the military."

Fighting for the U.S. in World War II

Manong "Peping," a World War II veteran, is a passionate voice for the Filipino soldiers who fought under the American flag alongside American soldiers. He speaks as a veteran who experienced some of the most horrific aspects of the Pacific war.

In 1939-40, Japanese and U.S. relations worsened. In July 1941, President Roosevelt ordered the Commonwealth Army of the Philippines and U.S. Armed Forces in the Philippines to be merged forming the U.S. Army Forces in the Far East (hereinafter, USAFFE). Under the command of General Douglas MacArthur, the USAFFE was composed of 19,000 U.S. army soldiers, 12,000 Philippine Scouts, and 118,000 Commonwealth of the Philippines soldiers.

Manong Peping was 19 years old in 1941. He became part of the USAFFE as a Commonwealth soldier in September 1941.

The Japanese began its air attack on the Philippines on December 8, 1941, one day after the attack on Pearl Harbor. The Japanese land invasion followed. Unable to stop the Japanese, MacArthur withdrew to the Bataan Peninsula and the island of Corregidor. In making their hasty retreat most of their supplies were lost, yet they continued to fight. President Franklin Roosevelt, in a radiogram to General Jonathan Wainright, who commanded the USAFFE, stated that:

"In every camp, in every naval vessel, soldiers, sailors, and marines are impressed by the gallant struggle of their comrades in the Philippines. The

workers in our shipyards and munitions plants redoubled their efforts because of your examples. You and your devoted followers become the living symbol of our war aims and the guarantee of our victory."

Manong "Peping's" squad was among the troops given the task of defending Bataan and Corregidor. Their resistance delayed the Japanese advance for four months, and kept a large Japanese army tied up in the Philippines long after Malaya, Singapore and the Indies had fallen.

Bataan Death March

The soldiers of the USAFFE fought valiantly against tremendous odds. But with no reinforcements and no food and ammunition, the decision was made to surrender. So on April 9, 1942, the Filipino and American soldiers on Bataan formally surrendered to the Japanese army.

Manong Peping was one of the approximately 75,000 USAFFE soldiers who then became prisoners of war (POWs).

He and the others were forced to march to the destination that was to be their prison, Camp O'Donnell. The captured soldiers experienced unspeakable brutality over the forced five to seven day, 60-mile walk. No food, no water was the least of their suffering.

Manong Peping recalls soldiers beaten or bayoneted to death, or simply killed for falling out of line. Many prisoners of war were also overcome by dehy-

PHOTO: *Above, U.S. troops surrender to the Japanese at Corregidor in the Philippines, May 6, 1942. A total of 11,500 Americans and Filipinos became POWs, including the commander, Lt. Gen. Jonathan Wainright.*

Map below, 78,000 Allied Prisoners of War (POWs) — 12,000 U.S. and 66,000 Filipino soldiers — are forced to walk 60 miles. The Japanese treated the POWs with extreme cruelty resulting in 11,000 deaths.

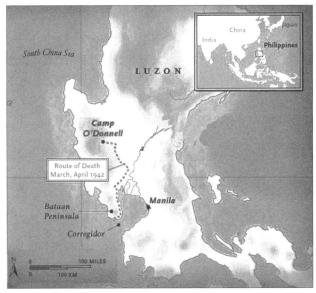

MAP COURTESY OF THE CORREGIDOR HISTORIC SOCIETY

dration, exhaustion, and disease. The exact number of deaths on the march is difficult to assess, the death toll ranges from 5,000 to 10,000 Filipino and 600-650 American POWs.

Surviving in the POW Camp

"It is less painful to remember the atrocities and brutalities of the war than to think of the denial of our military service in the U.S. Armed Forces."

– Manong "Peping" Baclig

Arriving at the prison camp, conditions were no better. Hundreds of people were packed in bamboo houses that were designed for far less. There was no medicine. In camp, Manong Peping recalls "death everywhere" — 300 to 400 POWs died each day and eventually over 23,000 POWs died of dysentery, malaria, typhoid fever and other tropical diseases.

He vowed to himself that if he ever got out of the death camp, to work for his fellow man. Although Manong Peping was not a religious man at the time, he "found his own redemption" tending to the injured and dying POWs in the Bataan death camp.

On June 6, 1942, the Filipino soldiers were granted amnesty by the Japanese military and released. The American prisoners continued to be held. Instead of returning home, Manong Peping decided to continue to fight. He became a guerrilla. He was one of the valiant soldiers who made the Philippines one of the hardest fought resistance movements in Southeast Asia. These anti-Japanese guerrilla forces were scattered all over the Philippine islands and were strategically indispensable to the Allied war effort in the Pacific.

After the War: The Battle for Veterans' Equality

"It is less painful to remember the atrocities and brutalities of the war than to think of the denial of our military service in the U.S. Armed Forces."

– Manong "Peping" Baclig

Stricken with malaria, Manong Peping eventually recovered. He came with his family to America on June 16, 1986. He was 64 years old. A year later, he became a naturalized citizen. Ironically, the date was December 7, 1987.

As he grew older, he became more concerned about health benefits and found that even as a U.S. citizen he was unable to apply for U.S. veteran benefits. Manong Peping had served the U.S. and his homeland as a Commonwealth soldier and as a member of the guerrilla force and had endured many hardships

PHOTO: AMERICAN COALITION FOR FILIPINO VETERANS, INC.,

Photo: Filipino veterans demonstrating in front of the White House on July 21, 1998 to appeal to the president to recognize the military service of Filipino WWII veterans.

but he and his comrades were denied benefits that were promised.

Manong Peping was very angry. The passage of the Rescission Act of 1946 had denied Filipino soldiers the veterans' benefits they had been promised. He considered this as a grave case of injustice and lack of equity. The only difference he saw between the American soldiers he fought and sat beside in WWII was the color of his skin — brown. He decided to seek justice — to fight for what had been promised.

The Long Struggle

Aging Filipino veterans wanted the United States to live up to its promise to them and embarked on a crusade to gain recognition and their rights. The struggle has been long and marked by a series of hard won victories. Manong Peping has been in the midst of these efforts.

He worked for the passage of the Immigration Act of 1990 that recognized active military services with the USAFFE for naturalization purposes only. This legislation was a crucial victory. The law recognized the World War II role of Filipino veterans and granted them U.S. citizenship on the basis of that service. Since the passage of the law, more than 30,000 aging Filipino WWII veterans have become citizens.

However, even as citizens, Filipino veterans were still not eligible for VA benefits and many lived on their SSI payments. Realizing the need for greater awareness of the difficulties faced by Filipino veterans, Manong Peping and Manong Franco Arcebal organized the American Coalition for Filipino Veterans (ACFV). They organized conferences and coalitions to focus on the inclusion and recognition of Filipino veterans as U.S. veterans and to secure the benefits awarded in the GI Bill of Rights. Many Filipino Americans as well as the general American public did not know the role played by Filipino soldiers in the USAFFE, the Bataan Death March, and the history and the exclusion of Filipino veterans following the war — so creating awareness was a critical step.

Creating Awareness — Gaining Support

Many Filipinos who were in the "Old" Philippine Scouts, which later were incorporated in the U.S. Army, were recognized as veterans after WWII and awarded with American citizenship and the full list of veteran benefits.

> *"The only difference he saw between the American soldiers he fought and sat beside in WWII was the color of his skin — brown."*
>
> – Casimiro Tolentino

The GI Bill

The GI Bill was enacted in 1944 and helped to transform the United States through its educational benefits. Also important were the benefits provided for health, disability, burial benefits, and to widows/dependents. These benefits are coordinated by the Department of Veterans Affairs (VA) and historically available to former members of the different branches of the U.S. military.

"Manong Peping is a passionate voice for the Filipino soldiers who fought under the American flag alongside of the American soldiers."

– Casimiro Tolentino

But Manong Peping and Manong Franco as Commonwealth soldiers who fought side by side with their Filipino and American comrades in Bataan, were denied the same GI Bill benefits. On June 14, 1997 Manong Peping and other Filipino veterans began a round the clock vigil at the statue of General MacArthur in MacArthur Park in Los Angeles to publicize their struggle. State and local legislators joined in the "camp out" and supported the need for "equity and justice" for the veterans. California quickly passed veterans benefits of $181 per month.

Manong Peping also organized other demonstrations in Los Angeles, New York, San Diego, and Washington, D.C. to "educate and agitate our community." He spent the next years flying from his home in Los Angeles to Washington, D.C. to lobby Congress and policy makers. He understood the importance of gaining the support of state and federal legislators.

Congressman Bob Filner (D-San Diego) was one of the early supporters of the Filipino veterans. Congressman Filner in September 1997 joined Manong Peping and other veterans who chained themselves in front of the White House to bring attention to the issue.

Demonstrators were arrested and fined $50 each. They were successful in bringing attention to the failure of Congress to pass a bill that would have given the Filipino veterans equity with American veterans.

In 1999, Filipino veterans won passage of the Special Veterans Benefit Law allowing veterans to take 75% (approximately $400 of their monthly Social Security benefits) when they return to the Philippines and Full Service Connected Compensation Benefit.

With the passage of (PL 108-170) signed by President George Bush in 2003, Filipino veterans were another step closer to their goal. This law provided official recognition and Veterans Administration (VA) medical care for approximately 11,000 Filipino WWII veterans living in the United States.

But Manong Peping continues to seek recognition and justice for all Filipino veterans. Today, there are still approximately 30,000 Filipino WWII veterans who reside in both the Philippines and the United States. He and the other veterans want the U.S. government to recognize their service as part of the United States armed forces during WWII. They seek the full veteran's benefits from the U.S. Department of Veterans Affairs (VA) promised them and a monthly permanent disability pension if they are poor and disabled. Many of these Filipino veterans have died, many are now aged (many are over 80 years of age),

"Manong Peping's efforts honor both the veterans of America's "great generation" but also the younger veterans fighting in the Middle East."

– Casimiro Tolentino

PHOTO COURTESY OF FAUSTINO BACLIG

ill and disabled. It is for these comrades that Manong Peping has dedicated his time and energy. He wants them out of exile and given the hard earned "equity" due to all those who fought under the American flag.

Recognition At Last

In April 2008, the U.S. Senate passed S.1315 that awarded pension benefits to Filipino veterans living in both the U.S. and in the Philippines. The vote was 96 to 1.

Then-Senator Barack Obama was a strong supporter of the bill, noting:

"This legislation also makes good on our promises to Filipino veterans who served bravely alongside American service members during World War II. Nearly 250,000 Filipinos assisted Americans during the war, but for far too long these heroes have been denied benefits they are owed. This bill will finally provide surviving veterans and their survivors with the benefits they were promised so many years ago."

The bill, however, needed the approval of the House of Representatives and the signature of the president to become law. Unfortunately, in the House, the bill experienced opposition and in the end, the House did not vote on the bill.

In the last days of the 2008 session, Congress turned its focus to the economic meltdown of the country and prospects for passage of any legislation on behalf of the Filipino veterans looked grim.

The new year 2009 brought a new President, Barack Obama and a new administration. On February 17, 2009 the first major piece of legislation, HR 1, the American Recovery and Reinvestment Act of 2009, the economic stimulus bill, was signed into law. Realizing that the ranks of the Filipino veterans were thinning, legislative supporters included a provision for the aging Filipino veterans in HR 1. The provision recognizes the military service of Filipino soldiers as U.S. veterans, and additionally provides one-time payments of $15,000 to Filipino American veterans residing in the U.S. or in the Philippines, and $9,000 to veterans who are Philippine citizens. It also contains a provision for spouses and protects eligibility for benefits currently received by veterans. Though not the benefit package sought by the veterans, it must be seen as victory in extremely difficult economic times. Manong Peping recognized the legislative supporters noting:

"Speaker Pelosi's support was critical in moving this in the House. We thank her, as well as Rep. Mike Honda and the Congressional Asian Pacific American Caucus, as well as Rep. Xavier Becerra for keeping this issue alive. House Veterans Affairs Committee Chairman Bob Filner's support for this issue has also helped bring us to this day."

Signing of the bill was a belated birthday present for Manong Peping who celebrated his 87th birthday on February 14, Valentine's Day. This is the last chapter of Manong Peping's long struggle for justice. His efforts honor both the veterans of America's "Greatest Generation," and the younger veterans fighting in the nation's current wars. He continues to inspire younger community activists showing them that perseverance for a good cause has no boundaries. Manong Peping truly embodies the spirit of the "Fighting Filipinos."

Chapter 5

Americans after September 11, 2001

"We are a nation of immigrants, yet we are also a nation that goes through evil cycles of anti-immigrant fervor."

–Bill Ong Hing

. . . .

"If I didn't act, then my family members and friends were going to be that much more likely to face similar discrimination later in their lives."

–Amric Singh Rathour

"After Words: September 11, 2001"
(to a rap of your own making)

Today, it's another city, they say.
Another New York. Another L.A.
Another America changed forever.
Newscaster, generals, and presidents say.

Today, it's another city, they say.
Bring Third World terrorists to justice.
Look for someone slightly darker
   (than even me)
Maybe a guy not so slant-eyed, taller,
Who speaks Arabic or Farsi,
Not Chinese or English.

Today, it's another city, they say.
He, or she, or they, may be praying or plotting
In a Mosque. In a Temple. In a Church.
In a truck, car, or plane.

Today, its another city, they say.
Nah. Mexicans don't qualify as the enemy.
They just hop borders, everyday, they say.
Not even Chinese, or Russians are enemies
Isn't that another place, another time?

Today, it's another city, they say.
But what if the enemy lurks within?

Within the alley of the aorta.
Within the barrio of the brain.
Within the gutter below the skin.
Within the bullet of the eye.
Within the twist of the blade
Within your back?

Look me straight in the eye, I say.
Dead or alive, I'm a different person
Than who I was yesterday.

            — Russell C. Leong

From "*Asian Americans on War and Peace*", edited by Russell Leong
and Don Nakanishi (UCLA Asian American Studies Press, 2002).

Who Took the Rap? A Call to Action

Russell C. Leong

Each decade challenges Americans to once again examine their own experiences and responses to crisis,
to their constitution, and to their civil rights. When
the twin towers of the World Trade Center collapsed on
that fateful September 11, 2001 after being hit by hijacked
American airplanes, ordinary Americans like you or me
reacted strongly.

Who Took the Rap?

Unfortunately, complex feelings of grief, anger, revenge,
and disbelief were often targeted at brown-skinned people
of Arab, Asian, or even Latino descent living in the U.S., or
at those who were wearing a turban or perceived as Muslim. Hate crimes, beatings, and indiscriminate epithets
directed against individuals and groups associated with
Arab, South Asian, and Islamic communities occurred in
cities and towns throughout the nation. Many politicians,
mass media, and even some lawyers proposed the curtail-
ment of some civil, and even constitutional rights in the
aftermath of 9/11.

Should Americans Accept Racial Profiling after 9/11?

According to Asian American journalist Helen Zia, "each day after September 11 has brought on some new uncertainty — and some new erosion of the principles that have made our country great. Yesterday, it was the argument of Peggy Noonan, a *Wall Street Journal* columnist who claimed that we must all 'accept the necessity of racial profiling.' She said that all Americans have to sacrifice some of our liberties in this post-September 11 world."

Do you agree or disagree with Noonan?

I, for one, do not agree, and it's not because I am Asian American, or that I work as an editor or as a teacher at UCLA. Bottom line, I believe that extraordinary times of social danger and instability demand even stronger, and "extra" protection to ensure the constitutional rights and civil liberties of all those who live in America. We must all work harder to achieve this.

True, all Americans are living in extraordinary times with pressures and the conflicts of war, the economy, and politics that challenge our day-to-day lives and thinking. Nonetheless, we must turn our fears into hope and our hope into action to protect what America stands for, including the civil, legal, and human rights of all those who now live in America.

Americans therefore cannot accept being racially, religiously or ethnically profiled — just because of the color of their skin, their immigration history or their religion.

And can Americans stand by while the civil liberties of others are taken away, violated, degraded or disregarded?

Ask yourself this question.

This is just what Bill Ong Hing, a law professor at UC Davis, did in his article, "Defending the Unpopular Immigrant." In his essay he talks about representing and working with persons and families that are "among the most unpopular groups in the United States today — undocumented immigrants from Mexico and legal residents who have been convicted of crimes."

Why Choose Justice Over Discrimination?

As Hing states, "we are a nation of immigrants, yet we are also a nation that goes through evil cycles of anti-immigrant fervor."

Bill Hing is an Asian American who is very much a typical American. He was born in the small town of Superior, Arizona, a small copper mining community that is mostly Mexican American. Bill's first languages were Spanish and English, and his Mexican neighbors reminded him of the Chinese migrants he had grown up with and known as well. In his work as a lawyer, Bill often represents Spanish-speaking clients, both immigrant and undocumented individuals alike in their quest for freedom and justice.

As a young immigration attorney, Bill worked in San Francisco, and there worked with many so-called Asian gang members from ordinary working class families. In the 1990s, he also represented clients from Southeast Asia, Cambodia, specifically.

After September 11, 2001, however, immigrant communities, both legal and undocumented individuals of Arab, Sikh, Pakistani, and Latino descent, were targeted. Hate-motivated incidents and hate crimes directed at these groups increased. In this atmosphere, those former gang youth and those who had been convicted of any felony crime were also targeted for deportation even after they had served their time.

Bill Hing strongly believes everyone deserves a second chance, and no person or family should be profiled because of their race, religion or current immigration status. As an immigration attorney, Bill works to assure that all are given the opportunity to secure justice and freedom.

> *"We must turn our fears into hope, and our hope into action."*
>
> — *Russell Leong*

How do South Asian Americans Create Community?

The 9/11 attacks triggered a new backlash of discrimination and violence against members of Arab, Muslim, and South Asian American communities. These attacks occurred throughout the U.S.: from Manhattan to San Jose, from Tulsa to Providence, R.I., to Gary, Indiana to Salt Lake City, and elsewhere. Sikh Americans, often mistaken as Muslim due to their wearing of turbans and beards as part of their religion, were, according to Karen Narasaki, "the victims of 133 reported hate crimes in just the first five days following the September 11 attacks."

In her essay, Narasaki, executive director of the Asian American Justice Center, documents the case of Amric Singh Rathour, an American-born Sikh. Most Americans are unaware of this small, yet vibrant South Asian community... a community that experienced post-9/11 discrimination and violence because of mistaken identity. The Sikh religion traces its origin to Punjab, located in present-day Pakistan and northern India. Sikh men wear turbans as part of their religious faith. This reading focuses on the issue of religious discrimination and one man's challenge to confront discrimination in the workplace.

Amric Singh Rathour wanted to practice his religion and be a New York police officer. He learned the importance of reaching out to others and gaining their support. During the case, Christian, Muslim and Buddhist leaders showed public support for Rathour. The Sikh Coalition, founded to protect Sikhs after 9/11, also helped by garnering the support of law agencies throughout the world in which turbaned Sikhs have been part of the police force including the Los Angeles County Sheriff's Department, the Royal Canadian Mounted Police, and the London Metropolitan Police. Finally, Rathour won his case because of support by a broad range of religious and civil rights groups.

Rathour's case was not the only one of discrimination against Sikhs after September 11, 2001. Nonetheless, by taking action to safeguard his civil rights, he was helping to pave the way for other ordinary Americans to safeguard their own legal and societal rights.

Can Youth Stand Up Against Racial, Religious and Sexual Profiling?

Today, all across the U.S., young people in high schools and colleges are becoming involved in their own communities and standing up for the civil, religious and legal rights of others in relation to what they believe. They are challenging the racial stereotypes and profiling of many groups, including Latinos, African Americans, Native Americans, Pacific Islanders, Asians, Arabs and Muslims, gays and lesbians, and even of stereotypes of themselves as a "Generation Y."

They are talking and marching as well as making their own music, writing their own lyrics and messages, posting their own ideas and feelings on the internet.

For today, music and culture can play a crucial role in powerfully shaping peoples' ideas about the present and the future. As writer and former UCLA student Jeff Chang says: "The hip-hop generation can play a crucial moral role in the call for peace — peace on the streets where we live and a global peace free from terror."

To better the world through rap. So, to all American youth, I would like to dedicate the poem I wrote above on September 11, 2001. I truly believe that words, music, and stories can also lead us to the path of liberation from fear and terror. Words and music can move the spirit and link our actions through space, time and generation.

There are many untold stories and new heroes for this generation. What is YOUR story? How will you tell your story? And how will you turn ideas into actions?

"Can Americans stand by while the civil liberties of others are taken away, violated, degraded, or disregarded?"

— Russell Leong

Photo: Felipe Cabral with daughters. Photo courtesy of the Cabral family.

Defending the Unpopular Immigrant

BILL ONG HING

Undocumented immigrants and immigrants con-victed of crimes have never been very popular. I recall an old book titled *Attorney for the Damned* about the famous courtroom attorney Clarence Darrow, who represented some very unpopular people during his career. I'm certainly not a Clarence Darrow; however, over the course of my career, my time in immigration courts has been spent representing and working with individuals and families that are among the most unpopular groups in the United States today — undocumented immigrants from Mexico and legal residents ("green card" holders) who have been convicted of crimes. We are a nation of immigrants, yet we are also a nation that goes through evil cycles of anti-immigrant fervor. But even in the best of times, the so-called "illegal" immigrants and criminal aliens don't have much support in the eyes of the public.

La Migra Bangs on the Door at 4 a.m.

The Cabral family moved to San Jose, California, in 1974 from Mexico, about the time I was graduating from law school. The father of the family, Felipe, was a baker in a local panaderia, a Mexican pastry shop. Lucrecia, the mother, was a stay-at-home mom, and they had four children — two daughters and two sons. The family entered illegally by paying a smuggler to help them cross the border, in Felipe's words, to seek "a better life." But a couple years later, someone — a "friend" or enemy or neighbor or co-worker — reported them to federal immigration agents, *la migra*, as they are called in the Mexican community.

The arrest was rude. It came at four in the morning, when agents surrounded the house and pounded on the front door. After several minutes, Sylvia, one of the daughters, answered the door and denied that anyone else was home. But the agents busted in, and eventually found the rest of the family hiding under the house. Everyone was arrested and dragged into federal detention. This was on May 20, 1976, and a couple days later I met the Cabral family when I was doing my rounds as a legal services attorney assigned to interview immigrants who had been taken into custody by *la migra*. Another daughter, Maria Reyna,

who was seventeen at the time of the raid, recently told me that "the incident was the most terrifying and traumatic experience of [her] life." For a long time, Maria Reyna "couldn't sleep and was often depressed."

Undocumented Under Federal Law

We have the power to exclude, to punish and to criminalize these border crossers. But that power must be implemented morally and ethically with an understanding that we are dealing with real human beings.

Unfortunately, there wasn't a whole lot that could be asserted on behalf of the Cabral family given the lack of rights provided to undocumenteds under federal law. In those days, it was easy enough to convince an immigration judge to allow Lucrecia and the children out of custody pending the deportation hearing, and Felipe was also released after the family came up with $2,000 bail. So at least, the family was out of custody as we prepared for the deportation hearing.

I remember visiting the family in San Jose on a Sunday afternoon to prepare for the hearing. They showed me around the house and the trap door that family members had used to hide under the house. They were upset about how the agents pushed their

"We are a nation of immigrants, yet we are also a nation that goes through evil cycles of anti-immigrant fervor."

— Bill Ong Hing

Photo: Felipe Cabral, at work at a Mexican bakery in San Jose, California.

PHOTOS COURTESY OF THE CABRAL FAMILY

way into the house at 4 a.m. and wanted to at least develop a strategy where they could complain about that behavior at the hearing. We decided that at their deportation hearing, they would refuse to admit deportability, thereby setting up a procedure where we could object to the introduction of their statements at the time of arrest on the grounds that they were questioned during an illegal search and seizure by the agents. We knew that that wouldn't get too far, but at least the family would be able to testify and complain about the conditions of the arrests. That was important to them.

The Cabral family took me in from the start. They were like the families that I grew up knowing, loving, and respecting in my hometown of Superior, Arizona, a small copper mining community in central Arizona that is predominantly Mexican American. The Cabral family, like the dozens of other families I knew in Superior, was kind, warm-hearted, friendly, hard-working, and decent. The children were fun-loving; the parents committed to their children, neighborhood, and church. They were in the United

FELIPE CABRAL *with daughters, above photo and with great-granddaughter, below.*

States to share a part of the American dream, not unlike the Gold Mountain image of America that Chinese migrants I knew had as well.

Although the immigration judge was not sympathetic and ruled against the Cabrals, the family was passionate about their plight. So much so, that over the next decade I made special motions on their behalf, filed administrative and judicial appeals (including one to the U.S. Supreme Court), and tried to get Congress interested in their case. Fortunately, in 1986, Congress enacted the Immigration Reform Control Act, which granted legalization (amnesty) for undocumented individuals who were in the United States for at least five years, and the Cabral family was able to obtain legal status. Felipe recently passed away, but I'm still in touch with the rest of this great *familia*. Maria Reyna, who now has her own family and works full time for Chrysler, volunteers on evenings and weekends for an immigrant rights organization in Redwood City, California. This is her way of helping others who are now facing what her own family endured.

"We have the power to exclude, to punish and to criminalize these border crossers. But that power must be implemented morally and ethically with an understanding that we are dealing with real human beings."

— *Bill Ong Hing*

Runnin' in Chinatown

Okay, so I really didn't know much about San Francisco Chinatown when I started going to law school in San Francisco in 1971. Going to school at Berkeley from 1967 to 1971 helped a little because I got to know many students who grew up in San Francisco, and especially when I started dating my future wife who grew up in the Chinatown/ North Beach part of town. The summer of 1972, after my first year of law school, I had the opportunity to spend all of my time in Chinatown working part time in two different places — the Chinatown YWCA kids summer camp and the neighborhood branch of San Francisco Neighborhood Legal Assistance Foundation (SFNLAF).

Photo: San Francisco Chinatown. © Russell Leong.

The work at the YWCA was especially educational for me when it came to beginning to comprehend what it was like growing up in Chinatown. While I was at the YWCA only for that summer, I had been at SFNLAF for eight years as a law clerk and attorney. Down the hall from the SFNLAF office, was the Youth Guidance Center, a gang counseling organization, so I couldn't help but get to know the counselors and many of the young men and women who hung out in the building.

I met many young gang members in a more official capacity as a young immigration attorney at SFNLAF. One was John Suey.

Child Immigrant — John Suey

John was born in Hong Kong, one of six kids. His parents, originally from mainland China, immigrated to Hong Kong after 1949 when the Communist Party took over. From there, the family was sponsored to come to the United States by John's aunt; John was seven years old. They settled in 1963 in San Francisco's Chinatown, where John's aunt owned a restaurant. John's parents worked twelve to sixteen hour days in the restaurant, mostly washing dishes. They were grateful for the opportunity to work and earn money, but found themselves too tired to spend much time with their children. Their search for other work was limited because they couldn't speak English.

Troubles Begin

The family was poor and the parents had to work long hours. The long working hours kept John's parents from providing much supervision as John and his siblings faced complicated cultural and economic adjustments. John's older siblings in high school started working part-time to help. John was the youngest boy in the family and had a lot of time on his hands. In grade school, he found companionship with neighborhood children who shared a similar background. Their parents were also busy struggling to get by. Like John these immigrant children also faced cultural and identity conflicts. John had trouble learning English and did not have much outside support for his studies. His parents did not know about tutoring and did not have the time to provide help in school. At school, the American-born Chinese (ABCs) children would pick on the foreign-born kids. This was more reason for John to hang out with children most like him. He did okay in school, but often got into fights with the ABCs. John did not see the rivalries as a racial thing, but simply the way things were in the neighborhood in which he grew up.

John gradually lost interest in school. On a typical day, he would go to school to meet his friends and cut classes. They started stealing from local stores for fun. Since his parents could hardly afford to give him any spending money, this became an easy and exciting way to get the small things he wanted. By selling what he stole, John made enough money to party, go out for dinner, and drink with his friends. Smoking, drinking and fighting became a regular occurrence in the neighborhood and John was caught participating in these activities several times. When John first started getting in trouble, his parents would hit him. It soon became clear that they could not control him, however, and they decided to allow the authorities to take John to a boys' home in Palm Springs after being sent to Juvenile Hall. He thought he would do better from then on, but John ended up in Juvenile Hall a total of eight times by the time he reached the age of eighteen, mostly for stealing, but finally for fighting.

The other kids in Juvenile Hall were of different races and bigger than John. John was forced to stand up for himself since he was constantly picked on by these larger kids. The counselors would give boxing gloves to kids who wanted to fight so they could settle their differences. By the time he was released John was tougher, and things got worse. He and his friends did not consider themselves a gang (they had no gang name and did not function like a typical gang). John only cared about having fun and making money, but his actions led to a conviction for armed robbery at age nineteen, and he spent three years at Soledad, a maximum security state prison.

John has said, "If you're not a criminal and you're sent to state prison, you become a criminal." John found himself in a place dominated by Blacks, Whites, and Latinos. This world taught him to sell drugs and offered him a heroin addiction. In Soledad, many of the inmates were serving sentences for murder. John was new and still a teenager, but the people around him had been there for years and enjoyed seducing younger inmates. Hardened by his previous experiences, though, John held his own as a "tough guy." No matter how tough he tried to be, John still knew he needed to ally himself with a group. With the few Asians, he made friends who would watch his back even as he did the same for them. At the same time, these friends exposed John to drugs. Each racial group had an organizer who negotiated and provided whatever the group needed. John was involved in several fights and spent most of his time in lock-downs and solitary confinement. After serving three years in state prison, he was released on parole for good behavior.

John spent six months at a halfway house. He received training in electronics and got a job at General Electric. Soon he was able to move out of the halfway house and rent an apartment in San Jose. The taste of freedom was sweet and he quickly wanted more. Since his family and friends were still in San Francisco, John started commuting frequently and visiting his girlfriend. John grew bored of working and tired of commuting from San Jose to San Francisco to see his girlfriend. He knew that moving back to his San Francisco neighborhood would expose him to strong temptation to return to his old habits, but he missed his family's home cooking and the support that he could only find close to those who knew and cared for him. After his parole ended, John quit his job with General Electric and returned to San Francisco. Back in his old neighborhood, he reverted to hanging out with old friends, using drugs and getting into fights. Prison had exposed him to heavy drugs, so that was what he sought. Without someone supervising his every action, it was almost like he did not know what to

> *"If you're not a criminal and you're sent to state prison, you become a criminal."*
>
> *– John Suey*

do with so much freedom. He quit his construction job and started distributing drugs for a drug dealer to earn money. Finally, he was caught and arrested.

In 1979, just two years after being released from state prison, John pleaded guilty in federal court to possession with intent to distribute heroin and was sentenced to two years. John spent the first twenty months in rehabilitation for his heroine addiction and learned that federal prison was much different from Soledad. In federal prison, many of the inmates were educated. They had not committed violent crimes, but were instead serving time for big time embezzlement, smuggling and the other white-collar crimes. The environment in the federal prison led John to think more clearly about what he was doing and where he was headed. He completed his GED while serving time and also attended a drug rehabilitation program. John was able to meet "a lot of good people." One of these was a 73-year-old man who became his friend and mentor. This man, an Asian minister, taught John to value his life and the life of others. John was forced to take a closer look at himself and realized the importance of self discipline. John learned of his mother's death while he was still in federal prison. This caused him to feel great remorse for what he had done and how he had missed being with those he loved. "It hurt me a lot. I [would always] return [from jail] badder and badder." Upon release in 1981, John, now age twenty-five, decided to do things right.

John was now married, and he was determined to stay out of trouble and to find steady work. Because he was an ex-felon, he was rejected over and over again, until an old friend helped him get a job at City Hall as a minimum wage clerk. After a year, he was accepted into a program for mechanic assistants.

Deportation Proceedings

While his life appeared to be on track, immigration officials took him into custody and initiated deportation proceedings because of John's criminal record. John had been in the United States for more than 25 years, and he thought he had paid for his crimes by serving time in prison. "I did my time, I don't deserve getting deported."

John became my client at SFNLAF just the way the Cabral family had, when I encountered him in custody at the local immigration holding facility. He was able to make bail of $5,000, and we began to prepare his case, knowing that his only chance was to persuade an immigration judge that he was now rehabilitated and deserved a second chance.

Since his initial immigration to the U.S. at the age of 7, John had never returned to Hong Kong. He knew no relatives or friends there and would have an extremely difficult time adjusting. His life, his home, his work and family were in the United States. In addition, John had become the sole provider and caretaker of his elderly father. Dozens of letters supporting John came from friends, family, a supervisor, co-workers, a parole officer and a court-appointed psychologist. John was a real partner in his case preparation, coming up with ideas on who could testify on his behalf and helping to gather letters of support. In 1985, John was granted a waiver of deportation by a stern immigration judge by establishing his rehabilitation and the likely hardship to himself and his family if he was deported. He was given a second chance to establish a life in the United States.

John not only maintained his status as a lawful permanent resident of the U.S., but applied and be-

Photos, opposite page and this page: Cambodian American youth, who participated in the little league team started by Many Uch.

came a naturalized citizen as soon as he was eligible. He continues to live in San Francisco and has worked with the municipal railway as a mechanic for twenty-five years now. He is married and has three teenage daughters. His children are his inspiration — he is clean from all drugs and works daily to keep his life on track. John is eternally grateful for everyone's help. I check in with John regularly, because he inspires me to keep battling for others who deserve a second chance.

From Pol Pot to Hot Pot

Many (pronounced the same as "Manny") Uch is a different sort of client of mine. You might say he's a policy client. What does that mean? Well, his case or situation represents a policy that I and dozens of others are trying to get changed. In 1996, Congress, in its wisdom, amended the immigration laws so that someone in John Suey's situation, namely an immigrant convicted of an aggravated felony, could no longer ask for a second chance. Now deportation is essentially automatic once you've been convicted of anything classified as an aggravated felony.

Many is one of these poor souls who was convicted of an aggravated felony after 1996, who has a pending deportation order. I first met Many through his federal public defender in Seattle, Jay Stansell, who told me about Many and how, while he was awaiting deportation he started a Little League Baseball team for some Cambodian youth in Seattle. That piqued my interest because I grew up playing Little League Baseball summer after summer in the Arizona heat, and I sent Many a $100 check so that he could buy some mitts for some of the young kids.

Early Life in Cambodia

At the age of seven, Many, his mother, and two older brothers came to the U.S. under horrific conditions. After their home country of Cambodia was pulled into war when the U.S. began bombing along the Vietnam/Cambodia border, the brutal Pol Pot-led Khmer Rouge regime came to power. Many's family was captured by the Khmer Rouge army, separated from their father, and forced from their home into the jungle. There they spent almost an entire year roaming and foraging for enough food to survive. In 1980, Red Cross workers found the family among the sick and the dead and placed them in a refugee camp.

Over the next four years the family bounced around from camp to camp, uncertain of their fate or of loved ones left behind. They assumed the worst. When Many's family made it to a refugee camp in the Philippines he began to pick up English and realized he was "a pretty smart kid." Yet life in the camps was dreary, and they were willing to sit through incomprehensible "Jesus movies" just to take their minds off tragedy.

On April 14, 1984, Many's family arrived in the United States as refugees. Their first destination was Richmond, Virginia, a place where nobody was like them. The family was scared and alone. In this strange new environment, they were placed in low-income housing, given a welfare check, and left to fend for themselves.

A year later Many's family decided to move to Seattle where other Cambodians they knew had been placed. There, living in a public housing project, they sought solace among others who understood their

"As the nation reeled from the September 11 attacks, Americans regrouped in incredible demonstrations of unity and patriotism. But an ugly side to that patriotism also emerged, targeting immigrant communities of Arab Americans, Muslims, Sikhs, and Pakistani Americans."

— Bill Ong Hing

trauma. Though these bonds helped, they could do little to assist Many when it came to actually succeeding in America.

Refugee Status

Refugees, Many says, "face many more obstacles than immigrants who voluntarily come here to work." Being forced from their homes to escape death, they are often unprepared for adjusting and still troubled by the nightmares of war. For Many, this abrupt move was especially tough coming from a country of very different traditions. Because his mother could not speak English and did not understand American customs, she could not advise him about school nor could she easily seek help from others. She had no formal education and most of the other elders had been farmers back home. None of them knew what dreams Many could have here.

Life at school was not much better for Many. He was placed in an "alternative school" that was completely unfit to teach him. "I didn't learn anything there, it was just too damn easy. They didn't expect anything from us, just to not cause any trouble." Half the girls were pregnant and almost all the guys were involved in something illegal. "How do I fit in with that?" he questioned.

Meanwhile in his neighborhood, Many faced the frustrations of poverty and discrimination. He always wondered why he couldn't have the things that other kids had. Kids at school would pick on Many for being different and poor. Riding the bus home from school, they would make fun of him for getting off in the "projects." They would also tell him to "go back to his country." Many didn't know how to respond, so sometimes he would get into fights over it.

In his elementary school English as a Second Language (ESL) class, Many befriended a group of guys from similar backgrounds who had similar problems. Growing up together they became very close. If other kids would pick on them, they would stand up for

each other. "If our friend got jumped, we didn't think twice. We'd go get those guys." Soon Many became trapped in this "tough mentality." If he didn't fight, the other guys might look at him as weak. Sometimes he would have to steal to prove himself. And if someone would get in trouble with the law, he would never snitch.

Many and his large group of friends went everywhere together. To him they were a much needed support group, but to police they were a gang. In the late 1980s when gang life in Los Angeles was being popularized, the label was pinned on Many and his friends. "We were never a gang, that title was given to us," he explained.

As Many grew older, life in the street became faster paced, and he found himself doing worse crimes to get by. Fighting and stealing became a way of life; Many felt he had no other options. "You don't really think you're wrong 'cause everyone in the neighborhood is doing the same things," he explained. As his life of crime escalated, Many found himself trapped. To get the increasing amounts of money he needed, Many began to get involved with drugs and guns. When Many was 18, he was convicted of robbery and sent to prison.

Over the next six years Many was in some form of detention. He spent more than three years in prison and over two in immigration detention. Ironically, it was here he would have the opportunity to cultivate himself in a manner that he was unable to in his neighborhood. Many took advantage of the opportunity. In prison he read books, went to school, and learned the law. Later he used this knowledge to petition for his release. After a tough battle, Many eventually won his freedom.

In many ways, Many is a unique success story of a criminal justice system that has all but abandoned rehabilitation as a goal. But since 2002, when the U.S. forced Cambodia to sign a repatriation agreement, the U.S. government has deported many refugee youth like Many. He finds such damage of breaking

PHOTO COURTESY OF BILL ONG HING

Bill Ong Hing, *lawyer and activist.*

"There's plenty of work today and tomorrow for anyone willing to serve as attorneys for the damned."

— Bill Ong Hing

up families unnecessary, especially after the debt to society has been paid through imprisonment.

Many has not let this threat stop him from working to improve lives of kids from his neighborhood who might fall victim to the same troubles he did. In addition to the Little League Baseball team he started, he tutors students at a local elementary school. "I want to show them the options nobody showed me. These kids relate to me because I know what they're going through."

Many's life now is quite different than it was before. He is now engaged to be married and runs his own delivery business. Growing up, Many never realized how tough life was in his neighborhood because his only other comparison was a life of war. Though he has prepared himself to be separated from his family once again, for others he says, "it would be a disaster." That's why he works tirelessly to help them. "I just wish someone would've gave me these tools back then, I really think I could have made it."

That's why I work with Many. Others and I continue to try to convince Congress to reinstate second chance possibilities that existed in the law prior to 1996.

The War on Terrorism

The tragic events of September 11, 2001, served as a reminder that the United States is a nation of immigrants that has grown more and more diverse since immigration laws were changed in 1965. As the nation reeled from the attacks, Americans re-

grouped in incredible demonstrations of unity and patriotism. But an ugly side to that patriotism also emerged, targeting immigrant communities of Arab Americans, Muslims, Sikhs, and Pakistani Americans. Hate speech and hate crimes directed at those groups surged, condoned largely by a governmental movement under the pretext of homeland security.

Targeting Arabs, Muslims, and South Asians in the United States began immediately after 9/11. U.S. Attorney General John Ashcroft authorized the immediate detention of 1,500 to 2,000 as "suspected terrorists," although none were ever charged with a terrorist act. Another 6,000 from countries identified as al Qaeda strongholds were arrested for ignoring court orders to leave the country. Then in late 2002, immigration officials mandated that everyone with a temporary visa from Iran, Iraq, Libya, Syria and Sudan had to report for new registration. This led to the unexpected detention of at least 450 individuals on technical immigration violations, many of whom had nearly completed the process for legal residency. Citizens of fifteen other countries, including North Korea, Saudi Arabia, Indonesia, Pakistan and North African nations, had to register by February 2003. Many of those were held in secret without access to family or legal counsel, deported even if minor immigration violations were found. In all, officials screened about 7,500 noncitizens under this effort, with none ever being charged with terrorism.

And so it goes. There's plenty of work today and tomorrow for anyone willing to serve as attorneys for the damned.

Photo: Sikh candlelight vigil at Central Park, New York City on September 15, 2001.

A Citizen Fights for His Civil Rights after 9/11: Amric Singh Rathour

Karen K. Narasaki

> *Every one of us has the capacity and the responsibility to step forward to protect our most cherished freedoms.*
>
> –Karen K. Narasaki
> President, Asian American Justice Center

In August of 2001, Amric Singh Rathour, a newly sworn-in officer of the New York Police Department (NYPD), was abruptly fired by his employer. The cause for Amric's termination was not any moral delinquency, but rather a violation of the NYPD's dress code. A practicing Sikh American, Amric was fired from his job because he refused to remove his turban while on police duty, an act that would have violated a major tenet of the Sikh religion. I understood personally the kind of suspicion, distrust and hostility these communities were facing. I myself am an American citizen of Japanese descent; my parents and their families were interned during World War II without due process despite the fact that they were also born here and also were citizens.

What I find inspiring about Amric's struggle to oppose the discriminatory uniform policy of the NYPD was the courage it took to assert his civil liberties at a time when individual rights were under siege and racial and religious discrimination were on the rise.

Weeks after Amric's termination, our nation suffered a great tragedy when terrorism struck our country on September 11, 2001. The terrorist attacks, however, triggered a new backlash of discrimination against members of Arab, Muslim and South Asian American communities. In 2001, there were 481 anti-Islamic hate crime incidents, a far greater figure than the 28 incidents that had occurred in 2000. Sikh Americans, often mistaken as Muslim due to their wearing of turbans and beards as part of their religious practices, were the victims of 133 reported hate crimes in just the first five days following the September 11 attacks.

Why Was an NYPD Police Officer Dismissed for Wearing a Turban?

Amric had a desire to serve his community. He decided to pursue this goal by becoming a New York City police officer. After passing his civil service exam, as well as a psychological and physical test, Amric was sworn in as a member of the NYPD.

When he began his police training, Amric was informed that the uniform dress code of the NYPD would not permit him to wear his customary turban. As a practicing Sikh, Amric wore a traditional turban in accordance with the observation of his religious faith. A police representative told Amric that instead of his traditional turban, he would have to wear a smaller turban under a standard issue officer's hat. As the training program continued, however, his superior officers began to express that even the smaller turban would not be acceptable.

Accepting his superior officers' previously stated position on the uniform policy, Amric believed he had the right to keep wearing his turban. He continued to wear his turban to police training sessions until one day his superior officers removed him from his class. "I was shocked that they would show so little respect to me, right in front of my fellow officers," Amric said. Amric was then placed in another room and told that he would not be able to join his fellow classmates until he removed his turban.

The next day, Amric returned to work wearing not only a turban, but the traditional, full-sized turban he had worn prior to the beginning of the training program. "At that point, I felt as though there was no point in changing how I practiced my religion if the police force was not going to honor its end of the bargain." His superior officers again removed him

---

Diversity in the United States: South Asian Americans

South Asian Americans represent a small but growing population within the United States. Although South Asian Americans comprise of less than one percent of the population, the South Asian American community has close to 2,000,000 members.[1] The group represents a diverse cross-section of ancestral national origins. More than 1,600,000 of the South Asian American community are of Indian descent. The next largest group is the Pakistani American community which has more than 155,000 members. Smaller segments of the South Asian American community are comprised of people with ancestry from Bangladesh, Nepal, Sri Lanka, Bhutan and the Maldives.[2]

The South Asian American community is a very diverse group spiritually as well. Members of the community practice a wide variety of religions, including Buddhism, Christianity, Hinduism, Jainism, Judaism, Islam, Sikhism and Zoroastrianism.[3]

1. Terrance J. Reeves and Claudette E. Bennett. "We the People: Asians in the United States." U.S. Census Bureau. Dec. 2004. 10 Sept. 2007. <http://www.census.gov/prod/2004pubs/censr-17.pdf>.

2. "Who Are South Asian Americans?" South Asian American Leaders of Tomorrow. 10 Sept. 2007. < http://www.saalt.org/pdfs/ Who_are_South_Asians.pdf>.

3. Ibid.

from his class and, soon after, the NYPD fired him from the police force.

The September 11 Attacks: Discrimination and Hate Crimes

Several weeks after Amric was fired from the police force, the terrorist attacks of September 11, 2001 tragically took the lives of nearly 3,000 people. The attack brought out the best and, sadly, also the worst in some people. Hundreds of hate crimes were perpetrated against Muslim Americans, as well as people who were mistaken to be Muslim.

Just four days after the terrorist attacks, the unthinkable occurred in Mesa, Arizona. On September 15, 2001, Balbir Singh Sodhi, a turbaned Sikh American, was murdered by an American citizen attempting to lash out against the Muslim community. Sodhi was targeted because of his turban, an article of clothing incorrectly considered by some to be exclusively associated with the Islamic faith. It was in this environment of prejudice and intimidation that Amric Singh Rathour, himself a turbaned Sikh American, faced the question of how to respond to the NYPD's termination of his employment on the basis of his religious observation.

Amric Singh Rathour: Practicing Sikhism in America

Amric had lived his entire life in the United States. Born in Queens, New York, Amric loved his country and his community. Amric was also very proud of his Sikh heritage. Sikhism is a religion of South Asian origin that promotes the values of devotion to God, truthful living and social equality for all. For male Sikhs, wearing a turban, or *dastaar*, is both a privilege and a critical responsibility of their faith. It serves as a constant reminder of their commitment to embody the tenets of Sikhism in their everyday actions.

Although there are more than 500,000 Sikh Americans in the U.S., many communities have few or no Sikh residents. As a result, there is little understanding of the Sikh religion and the people who practice it. As a result many Sikhs who wear turbans are often harassed. In many schools in the United States, turbaned Sikh boys are often teased by other students for dressing differently. As a child, Amric had experienced such treatment while attending elementary school in New York. As adults, Sikhs and

PHOTO COURTESY OF THE SIKH COALITION

"People should not have to choose between their work and their religion."

– Amric Singh Rathour

> "If I didn't act, then my family members and friends were going to be that much more likely to face similar discrimination later in their lives."
>
> – Amric Singh Rathour

Photo: Signs such as this were commonly posted on ranches and farms in the Phoenix, Arizona area. United Press photograph, February 6, 1935 reproduced from "Asian Americans on War and Peace", edited by Russell Leong and Don Nakanishi (UCLA Asian American Studies Press, 2002).

other religious and racial minorities continue to face racism, unequal treatment in the workplace and even the threat of physical violence. In the wake of September 11, these incidents increased dramatically.

Amric believed that becoming a police officer would be an ideal way to give back to his community and share the values of Sikhism, Amric quit his old job and began to prepare for the numerous tests he would need to pass to become a member of the New York Police Department.

Then the police department notified Amric that they had changed their position and decided that the wearing of any turban at all would violate the NYPD uniform code. He was shocked.

Because Amric and his wife were raising a newborn child at the time, this threat to his job security could not have struck at a worse time. Amric's plan for his family's financial security had been founded upon the police department's promise.

With his familial responsibilities, Amric had to decide how to respond to his firing. On one hand, he knew that he could simply give up, either by looking for a different job or agreeing to no longer follow his religious observation requirements.

On the other hand, by challenging the NYPD uniform policy before a court of law, Amric could assert his right to freely practice his religion without being subjected to discrimination at the workplace.

Taking Action against Discrimination

Amric faced the difficult decision. Initially, Amric was unsure of how to proceed. However, after he was fired from the NYPD, Amric learned of Jasjit Singh Jaggi, another Sikh American police officer who was faced with the same situation. Initially, Jaggi went along with the uniform code while he made a request for a religious exemption to wear his turban. However, when this request was denied, Jaggi resigned from his post rather than give up his religious obligation.

When Amric learned of this, he became more convinced that he should challenge the police department's uniform policy. Until then, he hadn't realized that other people might also be facing the same unfair treatment. Amric saw that the NYPD's policy as systematic discrimination against all Sikh Americans. With this knowledge, Amric saw the need for him to challenge the policy became more urgent. "I've known many Sikhs who have chosen to stop wearing a turban because of the mistreatment they have received from others in the workplace and in other social contexts," said Amric. "I've always believed that this was not right. People should not have to choose between their work and their religion."

Seeing that the challenge he faced was not specific to him, Amric also believed that he had a personal responsibility to take action. "I couldn't be dependent upon others to take a stand for my rights," Amric said. "If I didn't act, then my family members and friends were going to be that much more likely to face similar discrimination later in their lives."

Lastly, Amric also believed that in the post-September 11 environment it was more important than ever that Sikhs were represented on the police force. Sikh representation on the police force held the potential to both improve relations between the NYPD and the Sikh community and to serve as a symbolic reminder to the public of the contributions to the community that were made by Sikh Americans. For all of these reasons, Amric decided to take action against the NYPD's discriminatory uniform policy and fight for his former job.

Finding Allies for Activism

Although Amric had decided to appeal the police department's uniform policy, he was unsure of what steps to take next. Like most Americans, Amric had never before taken political or legal action to secure his rights. He had limited resources and no previous experience in activism.

Fortunately, Amric soon found a vital ally in a group called the Sikh Coalition. The Sikh Coalition — or the Coalition of Sikh Organizations, as it was known at the time — was founded immediately after September 11, 2001, in response to the flood of hate crimes which targeted Sikh as well as Arab and Muslim Americans after the terrorist attacks.

Anticipating the occurrence of more hate crimes against the Sikh community in the days to come, the Sikh Coalition organized affiliates across the country to encourage the government to take actions to protect Sikh Americans from violence and provide public advocacy services to members of the Sikh community who faced discrimination.

Sikhism

Sikhism is a religion practiced by more than 23 million people. Most followers of Sikhism are from the Punjab region of India, however Sikhs can be found around the world. In the United States, Sikhism is practiced by more than 500,000 people.

Sikhism is a religion based upon the principles expressed through the teachings of Sikhism's founding Ten Gurus. These principles include equality of all people before God, virtuous living and philanthropy.

Sikh Guru Nanak first laid the teachings of Sikhism out more than 500 years ago. Guru Nanak was followed by nine more Gurus who continued to preach the principles of Sikhism. The last Guru, Guru Gobind Singh determined that no more living Gurus were necessary to further the teachings of Sikhism. Instead, Guru Gobind Singh said that the spiritual manifestation of the Guru would henceforth be within the Sikh scriptures and the worldwide community of Sikhs.

In addition to the principles of Sikhism, practicing Sikhs also observe the maintenance of five articles of faith. The articles of faith are objects that Sikhs should always have with them as reminders of their responsibility to God and the teachings of Sikhism. The five articles are the Kesh, the Kangha, the Kara, the Kirpan, and the Kachh. The Kesh, or uncut hair, signifies human life in a natural state in harmony with God. This uncut hair must be covered by a turban that serves as a symbol of love for and commitment to Sikhism. The Kangha is a small comb worn to remove tangles from hair. Symbolically, it is meant to serve as a reminder to rid oneself of impure thought. The Kara is a steel bracelet meant to remind wearers of the service they owe to Sikhism. The Kirpan is a small religious sword meant to represent a Sikh's obligation to strive to be courageous and self-reliant. It also represents the obligation to have the strength and capacity required to defend those in need. Lastly, the Kachh is a type of under-shorts meant to remind Sikhs of their obligation to maintain self-restraint and high moral character.

ALLIES: *from above, Amric and wife Prabhjot Kaur Rathour; Sikh police officers from Canada and Great Britain; members of the Sikh Coalition.*

First Action Against Discrimination

When the Sikh Coalition learned of Amric's firing, the organization offered to provide free legal representation to him so that he could challenge the discriminatory NYPD uniform policy. Even with the legal assistance to go to court, however, Amric still faced an uphill battle. Amric's first action was to bring his case before the Equal Employment Opportunity Commission (EEOC), the federal government agency charged with the responsibility of ending employment discrimination in the United States. In December 2002, the EEOC ruled that the NYPD had not unlawfully discriminated against Amric by prohibiting him from wearing his turban.

In response to this setback, Amric and the Sikh Coalition redoubled their efforts. With the Sikh Coalition's experience in public advocacy, Amric was able to effectively tell his story to various media outlets. Many newspapers published stories and favorable editorials about his struggle to overcome the discriminatory effects of the NYPD's employment practices. Amric also pleaded his case directly to elected government officials. Through an online petition, he gained 6,000 signatures in support of his cause and sent them to the mayor of New York.

In addition, Amric and the Sikh Coalition reached out to other communities in order to build a larger coalition of support. Amric gained the support of law enforcement agencies from around the world in which turbaned Sikhs have been welcomed and functionally integrated within the police force, including the Los Angeles County Sheriff's Department, the Royal Canadian Mounted Police and the London Metropolitan Police.

In his struggle for religious freedom, Amric's support did not come exclusively from the Sikh community. Amric was joined in his efforts by a wide variety of religious leaders from all walks of faith. Christian, Muslim and Buddhist leaders showed public support for Amric and spoke out against his unfair treatment.

Filing a Federal Lawsuit

Finally, in March 2003, Amric and the Sikh Coalition filed a federal lawsuit challenging the NYPD's "no turban" policy. In support of his claims, Amric submitted testimony to the court from Sikh police officers from around the world in

"I've known many Sikhs who have chosen to stop wearing a turban because of the mistreatment they have received from others in the workplace and in other social contexts. I've always believed that this was not right."

– Amric Singh Rathour

opposition to the NYPD's uniform code. Soon after, the New York attorney general spoke out against the police department's ban on turbans. As support for Amric continued to grow among members of the media, elected officials and ordinary citizens alike, the prospect of a legal victory for Amric's right to wear a turban while on duty as a police officer became more and more likely.

Several weeks later, a decision in another lawsuit provided the critical push to help Amric win his cause. Jasjit Singh Jaggi, the Sikh American had also filed a legal challenge to the uniform code. In April of 2004, the judge presiding over Jaggi's case ruled that the NYPD's policy was a violation of its member officers' civil rights. After the decision, the police department declared that it would change its uniform code to allow for religious turbans and offered to reinstate both Amric and Jaggi back onto the police force. After three long years, Amric could finally serve his community and support his family while staying true to his religious principles.

Safeguarding Your Civil Rights

In America, threats to our civil liberties have taken different forms. The threats to civil rights in the United States after 9/11 are unique in the forms of the bigotry they have elicited and the people whom they have targeted. However, these new threats to civil liberties can only be overcome in the same way: by the actions of ordinary citizens — you and I — answering the call to safeguard all of our rights.

Today, Amric Singh Rathour continues to serve his community as a New York City police officer. As an officer, Amric has received the respect and support of his colleagues. Since his legal challenge to the police department's uniform policy, Amric has

remained active in the field of civic engagement by sharing his story and continuing to speak out against religious discrimination.

William Lauro and Aditi Eleswarapu, 2007 summer interns at the Asian American Justice Center, contributed to this article.

References:

Federal Bureau of Investigation. "Crime in the United States, Uniform Crime Reports, 2001." Washington, D.C.: U.S. Department of Justice. 2001.

"Hate Crime Reports Up in Wake of Terrorist Attacks." CNN.com. Sept. 17, 2001. Sept. 10, 2007. <http://archives.cnn.com/2001/US/09/16/gen.hate.crimes/>.

National Commission on Terrorist Attacks Upon the United States. "The 9/11 Commission Report." Sept. 10, 2007. <http://www.gpoaccess.gov/911/pdf/fullreport.pdf>.

Haidar, Suhasini. "Immigrants Fear Backlash to Terror Attacks." CNN.com. Sept. 19, 2001. Sept 10, 2007. <http://archives.cnn.com/2001/US/09/19/gen.hate.crimes/index.html>.

"Why Sikhs Wear a Turban." The Sikh Coalition. Sept. 10, 2007. <http://www.sikhcoalition.org/Sikhism11.asp>.

Prakash, Kanwal. "In Search of Rightful Place and Opportunity to Serve." SikhCouncilUSA.org. Sept. 10, 2007. <http://www.sikhcouncilusa.org/article.aspx?article=kpsinghdinner05>.

"Amric Singh – Equality Challenges Continue." The Sikh Coalition. Sept. 10, 2007. <http://www.sikhcoalition.org/ar2002_major_amric.asp>.

"Amric Singh – Federal Discrimination Lawsuit Against the NYPD." The Sikh Coalition. Sept. 10, 2007. <http://www.sikhcoalition.org/ar2003_major_amric.asp>.

Castellani, Anne. "Judge Rules in Favor of Turban-Wearing Officer." CNN.com. May 3, 2004. Sept. 10, 2007. <http://www.cnn.com/2004/LAW/04/30/turban.cop/>.

SikhCouncilUSA.org. Sept. 10, 2007. <http://www.sikhcouncilusa.org/article.aspx?article=kpsinghdinner05>.

"Sikhism at a Glance." The Sikh Coalition. Sept. 10, 2007. <http://www.sikhcoalition.org/SikhismGlance.asp>.

Chapter 6

Lessons for Students

"In elementary through high school, although I learned a lot about African American history through lessons on the Civil Rights Movements or the making of colonial America, none of my classes ever taught me about the histories of Chicanos/as, Latinos, American Indians, or Asian Americans."

– Irene Lee

. . . .

"I am extremely proud of my involvement in bringing Untold Stories to students. Too often the experiences and contributions of Asian Americans to the American story are absent from our textbooks. The lessons and historical timeline which I developed in Untold Stories are designed to fill that void. These are lessons of courage and strength of character, dedicated to the principle that justice and fairness should apply to all people."

– Esther Taira

아태법률센터와 UCLA 아시안 아메리칸 교육센터가 공동 출간하는 '언급되지 않은 시민 권리 이야기' 제작에
참여했던 아이린 이(왼쪽)씨와 스튜어트 쿼 사무국장이 책에 대해 설명하고 있다. 〈박상혁 기자〉

한인 등 소수계 영웅들 업적

학교에서 배운다

아태법률센터-UCLA 공동, 부교재로 출간
4.29 폭동 취재 이경원 기자 기록등 생생히

한인을 포함한 소수계 이민자 커뮤니티의 친정판 리더들의 이야기를 담은 고등학생 및 대학생용 부교재가 출간된다.

아태법률센터(APALC)가 UCLA 아시안 아메리칸 교육센터(AASC)와 지난 5년간 공동 진행, 마무리 발교작업이 진행 중인 '언급되지 않은 시민 권리 이야기'(Untold Civil Rights Stories)가 3월 정식 발간된 뒤 오는 4월부터 각 학급 내 부교재로 사용될 전망이다.

APALC의 스튜어드 쿼 사무국장은 "아시안 커뮤니티의 1.5세 및 2세들은 마틴 루터 킹, 시저 차베스 넬슨 만델라가 누구인지, 커뮤니티를 위해 어떤 희생과 봉사를 했는지는 잘 알고 있지만 정작 자신이 속한 아시안 커뮤니티의 리더가 누구인지는 모른다"라며 "이러한 학생들에게 올바른 이민 역사와 우리의 리더는 누구인자를 알리기 위해 교재를 만들게 됐다"고 설명했다.

이 책에는 4.29 폭동 농울 취재하며 한인 커뮤니티 목소리를 주요게 알리는 등 언론인으로 활약

한 이경원 기자의 업적을 담은 '인종간 다리 건설'(Building Bridges between Races), 학생의 눈으로 바라본 아시안 아메리칸 커뮤니티의 진정한 리더 등 아시안 커뮤니티의 이민생활 속에 나타난 주요 사건과 리더들을 자세히 소개하고 있다.

샌프란시스코 지역에서 성장, UCLA에 진학한 뒤 우연히 아시안 커뮤니티에 대해 관심을 갖게 됐다는 아이린 이(22)씨는 "고교 졸업 때까지 아시안 아메리칸에 대해 한 번도 배워본 적이 없었다"라며 "이번에 교재 준비 작업에 동참하면서 많은 사실을 알게 됐고 나와 같은 학생들이 더는 없기를 바라는 마음을 교재 속에 담았다"고 말했다. 〈김진호 기자〉

Photo: Korea Times story on 'Untold Civil Rights Stories' with Irene Lee, editorial intern and student, and Stewart Kwoh.

Student to Student:
The Rose That Grew From Concrete

IRENE LEE

"Did you hear about the rose that grew from a crack in the con-crete? Proving nature's law is wrong, it learned to walk without having feet. Funny it seems, but by keeping its dreams, it learned to breathe fresh air. Long live the rose that grew from concrete when no one else ever cared."
    –Tupac Shakur (1971-1996), *The Rose That Grew From Concrete*

What is a "hero"? If you asked me this question several years ago, my answer probably would have been something along the lines of "Super-man" or "Wonder Woman" — someone powerful, impor-tant and fearless. Back then, heroes were the characters you saw in comic books or TV shows. They were different from everyone else, and the only way you could be one was if you had lived inside the TV screen or within the pages of a pulp-fiction book.

"When I turned on the television to watch my favorite show, flipped open a magazine or studied for my next U.S. history test, Asian American faces and names just weren't there. I felt like the Asian American community was invisible in mainstream society."

– *Irene Lee*

I was born and raised in a small city called Hercules, located in the eastern part of Northern California's Bay Area. My parents, who immigrated to the U.S. in the 1970s, settled in California after they were married to raise my sister and me.

Like most first-generation immigrants, my parents were hard working, working-class, small business owners who went through a dozen different "mom and pop" stores by the time I entered high school. When I was younger, if I wasn't helping out at their stores, I rarely saw them during the week. For as far back as I can remember (and until this day), they worked seven days a week, fourteen hours a day to pay for the bills, put food on the table, and sent my sister and me to school.

My hometown was really small, really diverse, and had a large immigrant community. All throughout elementary to high school, my friends, classmates, and teachers were of all different ethnic and racial backgrounds. In high school, our entire student body consisted of mostly Asian American, African American and Hispanic students with a smaller number of white and other ethnic groups.

But even as multicultural as my community was at the time, I often felt detached from my own ethnic and racial identity as a Korean American/Asian American student. Why? Well, being born a second-generation Korean American, I felt like my values, beliefs and interests were different than my parents, for example, who were raised in Korea. I spoke mostly English at school and at home. I didn't like Korean food growing up (I know, insane, right?). And even though most of my closest friends were Asian, I found myself trying to avoid things or situations — like the "rice rocket" Asian racer crews at school or watching the Korean video rentals my parents would bring home every week — that made me look or feel too stereotypically Asian.

I didn't feel close to my Korean roots or Asian American identity — not because I was necessarily ashamed of it, but more because, back then, I didn't feel like I had a history or community to look up to and be proud of. Growing up, I felt that Asian Americans and other ethnic minorities didn't have much of a place in the media, in society or even in history textbooks. When I turned on the television to watch my favorite show, flipped open a magazine or studied for my next U.S. history test, Asian American faces and names just weren't there. I felt like the Asian American community was invisible in mainstream society.

In elementary through high school, although I learned a lot about African American history through lessons on the Civil Rights Movements or the making of colonial America, none of my classes ever taught me about the histories of Chicanos/as, Latinos, American Indians or Asian Americans. In history class, I wrote plenty of study note cards and five-paragraph essays on influential leaders like the Rev. Martin Luther King Jr. and President Franklin Roosevelt. But somehow, the names of figures like Fred Korematsu or Philip Vera Cruz never came up on an exam question or were even mentioned in assigned readings.

It wasn't until I took classes during college in ethnic studies that I began learning a whole other part to U.S. history — a part that honors the contributions of Asian Americans and other individuals of all different ethnic and racial backgrounds.

One of the first stories that I learned about in an Asian American Studies class was of the Vincent Chin case. I remember seeing a black and white photo of Lily Chin standing at the center of a stage, up at a podium, looking out into a crowd of people and images of her son's picture posted on picket signs behind her. This image immediately caught my attention because here was this first-generation Chinese woman who, at the time barely spoke English, but still found the courage to speak up against hate crimes and reach out to communities of all colors to come together and promote awareness. For me, this image spoke to the way people of color across the country share common experiences and can relate to one another, despite our different backgrounds or the misunderstandings we have about each other. Because when it boils down to sink or swim, do or die, all people of color in this country fight against the battle of being ignored and treated unequally.

After having learned about the experiences of more leaders like Fred Korematsu, Beulah Kwoh, or Philip Vera Cruz, the meaning of the word "hero" to me now has nothing to do with being different or more special than everyone else. Instead, it has everything to do with finding power in the most unlikely places and people.

In a society like ours, where everything from the color of your skin to the way you wear your hair could make you a subject of criticism, it isn't easy to find the courage to speak up for yourself and others. Martin Luther King Jr. once said that

faith is "taking the first step even when you don't see the whole staircase." In that case, I would say then that a "hero" isn't someone who has superhuman strength, a flapping cape or the ability to single-handedly rescue people from collapsing buildings. Heroes are not unlike you and me. They are ordinary people who make the extraordinary decision to stand up, against the odds, and fight for what they believe in and the people they love. The heroes of this book, like so many others throughout history, not only dared to dream up a better world, but also took action to find out what it would take to live in it.

So then, what makes an ordinary person a hero? It is the courage to jump in headfirst (while you don't always know where you'll end up), always remembering where you came from and never giving up on the hope for a better tomorrow.

Although each one of these heroes came from different walks of life, they share one simple but important thing in common. They were all just regular people who found the courage to fight for what they believed in. None of the heroes and civil rights leaders in this book came from a rich, famous, or even privileged background. Most of them were immigrants, part of the working class, and did not have the opportunity to pursue a higher education, like going to college. In a way, they were the underdogs of society, the anti-superhero. But still, these people were able to inspire national movements, overturn U.S. federal laws and make their issues, and the issues of others, known to the public.

"For me, this image spoke to the way people of color across the country share common experiences and can relate to one another, despite our different backgrounds or the misunderstandings we have about each other. Because when it boils down to sink or swim, do or die, all people of color in this country fight against the battle of being ignored and treated unequally."

– Irene Lee

PHOTO COURTESY OF P. A. LAVA, 2008.

"Heroes are not unlike you and me. They are ordinary people who make the extraordinary decision to stand up, against the odds, and fight for what they believe in and the people they love. The heroes of this book, like so many others throughout history, not only dared to dream up a better world, but also took action to find out what it would take to live in it."

– Irene Lee

Photo: Irene marching with fellow strikers at a Fall 2008 demonstration held in Long Beach, California, in protest of Proposition 8.

In spite of all the barriers they faced, these individuals refused to sit in silence while their voices, hardships and the people they loved were being ignored. And in their struggles, they not only fought for their own rights, but also crossed racial boundaries and reached out to different communities. For me, it is that kind of deep compassion for others and fiery determination that defines what a true hero is.

Remembering what the late rap artist and social activist Tupac Shakur said about the rose that grew from concrete, the failures and triumphs of these heroes remind me never to underestimate the power of my own voice. Like the rose, that defied nature's laws by blooming from a crack in the concrete, we have the power to defy our own odds and achieve what we want most. No matter how small or unimportant you or I might feel in this world at times, each one of us has what it takes to do something and be someone important in society.

The chapters in this book have more to do with than just letting you, the reader, learn about what these people were able to accomplish in their lifetimes. The story of each individual is a way for us to know of and be inspired by the heroes of our past, pass the torch, and find ways for you and I to understand what it means to inherit this legacy. In other words, the pages of this book should not be about memorizing bullet-pointed history facts, tucking that knowledge away in the back of our minds, and pulling it back out when an exam rolls around. Instead, it should be about taking in what we now know about the past, looking to the future, and discovering that we have the power to shape what that might look like in the years to come. You and I are a part of today's generation, society, and world. It is up to us to continue the legacy that leaders in history like Rosa Parks, K.W. Lee, Cesar Chavez and so many others have helped build.

You and I have the ability to do something important — right now, today — to make a difference in your life, others' lives, and our society. *The question is not whether or not we have the power to make change, but it is how we plan on doing it.*

What We Can Do

Take a step back and think about what is most important to you. What issues interest you and what can you do to get involved? Here are some ways you and I can make a positive difference in our own communities and society:

• **Get active on campus.** Find a club on campus that does activities that really interests you and join it. Be an active member and tell your friends about it! Joining a club that you're really into is a great way to meet other students that share the same interests and goals as you. Not only can you use your involvement in a school club to voice your opinions and become a part of an organized group, but you can also learn what it takes to set a goal, work with others, and find ways to help each other to achieve your individual and group goals.

• **Reach out into your local community.** Start by getting involved in your local organizations. For example, your local church, sports teams or community service groups are great places to start becoming an active member of the community and contributing to a great cause. By becoming active in local neighborhood groups, you can practice how to communicate with a group of people, voice your opinion, and become a better leader in your own community.

• **Volunteer for service learning projects.** Think about something you're really interested in and then find a place to volunteer for it. For example, if you really like working with younger kids, find a daycare or an after-school program that needs volunteers to work with kids in areas like math or English tutoring. That way, you can do something that you find fun and feel good about, while making a positive impact in someone else's life!

• **Get out the vote.** Voting and being involved in the political process is one of the most important ways that you can get your opinions heard. If you're of voting age and haven't registered to vote, go to your local DMV, Post Office, or other government office where you can fill out a registration form and get more information about voting. The mayor of your city, the laws that get passed, and the president of the United States of America is chosen based on your votes and mine!

• **Want to find other ways to make a difference?** While voting is an important way to make a difference in government policy, it is only one of the many ways you can get involved. Go research online, volunteer for a political campaign or write letters to your local government officials. Learn about what types of issues are affecting your community and find out what your mayor, governor or other local officials are doing about it. It is just as much our responsibility to make sure the officials we vote for and elect are properly addressing our communities' needs as it is to vote. The future of our cities and the types of laws that will affect us today and in the future is in our hands. So, stand up for what you believe in and make your voice heard. Your opinions and beliefs are important and can and do make a difference!

Lesson Plans and Resources

Prepared by Esther Taira

Lesson Title: Freeing Ourselves From Prison Sweatshops: Thai Garment Workers Speak Out

Unit of Study: Contemporary American Society

Grade Level: 11th Grade U.S. History; 12th Grade U.S. Government/Economics

History-Social Science Standards: Grade 11 U.S. History 11.11.7.
U.S. Government Grade 12 12.3.1 12.3.2 12.4.1.

Key Concepts:
Economic exploitation, change, community service, social justice, democracy, and leadership

Setting the Context:
In U.S. history, the term "sweatshop" is associated with the Industrial Revolution and the frightful conditions that workers had to endure at that time. In the minds of most, the passage of labor legislation has rectified this situation. This lesson highlights the enduring nature of the struggle for workers' rights. The lesson tells the story of seventy-two garment workers from Thailand who were forced to work behind barbed wire and under armed guard in an apartment complex in El Monte, California. Their release from enslavement in 1995 was only the first chapter in a story of courage and fortitude. The workers were then placed in federal detention, thus exchanging one kind of imprisonment for another. A number of community organizations (Thai Community Development Center, Korean Immigrant Workers Alliance (now the Koreatown Immigrant Workers Alliance), Asian Pacific American Legal Center, and Coalition for Humane Immigrant Rights of Los Angeles) came to the assistance of the workers revealing the importance of such organizations.

The complex workings of the garment industry are exposed as the garment workers seek justice through the courts. The Thai garment workers' lawsuit was the first federal lawsuit of its kind. Its objectives were two-fold: to get the workers paid for their long, hard labor and to challenge the entire garment industry that created the conditions for their abuse. Latino garment workers who also suffered from poor working conditions and low wages joined the lawsuit. In doing so, the workers had to overcome suspicion and distrust created by cultural and language differences.

The real world workings of the court system and the enactment of legislation are explored in this reading.

Expected Learning Outcomes: Students will be able to:

- Describe "sweatshop" conditions.
- Identify the labor practices that encourage "sweatshop" conditions.
- Explain the role of nonprofit organizations in championing the rights of workers.
- Identify the legal process used by the El Monte workers in seeking justice.
- Explain the pyramid-like structure of the garment industry.
- Describe legislation that now benefit garment workers.

Procedure

Guided Instruction:
Introduce the reading with a turn-of the century photo of a sweatshop. (Check out websites that focus on the Triangle Factory Fire such as the Cornell University site — *http://www.ilr.cornell.edu/trianglefire/photos/* for photos). Ask students to identify the scene. Pose the question: Are conditions like this still found in factories? Write the term *sweatshop* on the board. Ask for a definition — (a small factory or other establishment where employees are made to work very hard in poor conditions for low wages).

Expand the discussion to present day. If you have access to the internet, you may wish to visit "Between a Rock & a Hard Place: A History of American Sweatshops, 1820-Present." An interactive web site featuring photos and video clips of the El Monte Slave Sweatshop.

Assessment:
After completion of the reading, have students create a short role play of one of the key events in the experience of the Thai garment workers or using the experiences of the El Monte workers, answer the question: How can workers better protect their rights in the workplace? What governmental and community resources are available to them?

Extension Activities:
Students will be amazed with the number of organizations concerned with present-day sweatshops. Several sites are included here. Have students conduct additional research to find out the issues of concern today. Names of additional organizations are included. Have students complete comment column.

Name	Contact Information	Comment
Sweatshop Watch 310 Eighth Street, Suite 303 Oakland, CA 94607 Phone: 1-510-834-8990	Website: www.sweatshopwatch.org/ E-mail: sweatinfo@sweatshop-watch.org	"Sweatshop Watch is a coalition of labor, community, civil rights, immigrant rights, women's, religious & student organizations, and individuals committed to eliminating sweatshop conditions in the global garment industry. There is a newsletter archive that one can access to learn more about sweatshop activity.
United States Department of Labor 200 Constitution Ave., NW Washington, DC 20210 Phone: 1-866-4-USA-DOL (toll free)	Website: www.dol.gov/index.htm	This website contains a search feature which is almost necessary in this information-filled site. Sign-up for its e-mail list to receive updates and alerts. The website has an extensive archive of information on many different labor issues. One can see the government's point of view on assorted labor issues.
Add to chart		

Additional organizations include:
Stop Sweatshops: A Partnership for Responsibility UNITE!
United Students Against Sweatshops

Additional readings that focus on the lives of the El Monte workers.

Louder Than Words: Lawyers, Communities and the Struggle for Justice by Henda D. Hair. Rockefeller Foundation, 2001, Chapter 2 – "Client-Centered Lawyering: Garment Workers Advocacy in Los Angeles".

Sweatshop Warriors: Immigrant Women Workers Take On the Global Factory by Miriam Ching Yoon Louie. Published by South End Press, 2001, Chapter 6 – "Just in Time Guerrilla Warriors".

Service Learning: Los Angeles Unified School District has a lesson plan for a social responsibility and the global garment industry service learning project. Google Los Angeles Unified School District service learning, click on Teaching Aids or go directly to: *http://notebook.lausd.net/portal/page?_pageid=33,179449&_dad=ptl&_schema=PTL_EP.*

Reflection on Service Learning: After completing the activities students should take time to reflect and write their feelings on goals of the activity and the degree of successful completion; any personal feelings and experiences that occurred during the activity.

Activities

Vocabulary: Vocabulary terms and definitions.

Sweatshop
Nonprofit organizations
Coalition
Lawsuit
Litigation
Discovery
Depose

Identify:

Julie Su
Asian American Pacific Legal Center (APALC)
S-Visa
Assembly Bill 633

Focus Questions:

1. What motivated Jang, Jim, and Kaew, the three Thai women in the reading to come to the United States?

2. What did the federal and state law enforcement officers find in El Monte in 1995?

3. Who were the people the officers found and what were they doing?

4. Why did federal officials detain the workers?

5. Who were the nonprofit, community organizations that came to aid the workers? In what ways did they help the workers?

6. What is an S-Visa and why was it important to the El Monte Workers?

7. Why was it so remarkable that these garment workers chose to file a lawsuit?

8. Give two reasons why the lawsuit was important.

9. Describe the importance of Assembly Bill 633 to garment workers.

Lesson Title: United Farm Workers (UFW) Movement: Philip Vera Cruz, Unsung Hero

Grade Level: 11th Grade U.S. History

Unit of Study: Post-World War II America (1945-1960), Continuity and Change

History-Social Science Standards: 11.6.5; 11.10.5 5; 11.11.6

Key Concepts:
Civil Rights, nonviolent protest, change, community service, social justice, democracy, and leadership

Setting the Context:
This reading focuses on the struggle of farm workers to secure safe working conditions and a fair wage for the work they performed. Students should know that labor improvements were made in the 1930s but they did not include farm workers. Farm workers, for example were not covered by the 1935 National Labor Relations Act, which provided industrial workers the right to form unions and enter into collective bargaining. Nor were farm workers covered under the 1939 Fair Labor Standards Act, establishing a minimum hourly wage and maximum hours of work per week. As a result farm workers who performed grueling work, worked long hours for the very lowest pay. They had no union to represent them or protect them from unscrupulous employers or corrupt labor contractors.

During World War II farmers, especially those growing fruits and vegetables, relied on migrant workers, many were Filipinos and Mexicans. The life and efforts of César Chávez are generally the focal point of the textbook coverage of the organizing of farm workers. However, this information would be incomplete without acknowledging the contributions made by Filipino farm workers. This chapter shares the experiences of Philip Vera Cruz, a pioneer in the unionizing of farm workers.

Expected Learning Outcomes: Students will be able to:

- Explain the plight of farm workers — wages, working conditions, health hazards, etc.
- Describe the role of Filipino farm workers in the unionization efforts.
- Describe the role of the Agricultural Workers Organizing Committee (AWOC).
- Strategies used by farm workers in their negotiations for better pay and working conditions.

Procedure

Guided Instruction:
Introduce the reading by showing photos of migrant workers. Have students describe what they think it would be like to be a farm worker. Ask students to name the person most influential to the farm workers' movement. Cesar Chavez is the most likely individual that they will name. Explain that Filipino immigrants like Mexican immigrants found work as farm workers. Note that few people know the role played by Filipino farm workers in the union building efforts

If internet access is available in the classroom, go to the Farmworkers Movement Documentation Project website: click on media, click on photos and click on search — insert name of Philip Vera Cruz or click on *http://www.farmworkermovement.org/index.php* The site will give you a number of photos showing the close connection between Philip Vera Cruz who was the second vice-president of the United Farm Workers.

Conduct a guided discussion of the key events covered in the reading. A question-and-answer session after the students read and before they begin their assignment might help clarify some points. Students should be assigned to groups of 4 – 5 then given an assignment sheet.

Assessment:
The teacher will assess student understanding of these concepts through class discussion and by reading students' written answers to the questions.

Extension Activities

Students may research Philip Vera Cruz from *East Wind Magazine* (1982) *http://www.aamovement.net/history/eastwind/11/veracruz.html*

Review the United Farm Workers using the César E. Chávez website. *http://www.chavezfoundation.org/* How much information is included on the role of Filipino farm workers? Rewrite to provide a balanced historical perspective.

Philip Vera Cruz – A Personal History of Filipino Immigrants and the Farmworkers Movement by Craig Scharlin and Lilia Villanueva. University of Washington Press, 2000.

Movement history: Filipinos Build a Movement for Justice in the Asparagus Fields by Larry Salomon. Third Force [Volume 2, no. 4 (Oct. 31, 1994) p. 30].

Service Learning:

*   Students can complete the Migrant Farm Workers Project (LAUSD Service Learning Project).
*   Students will determine which are the most serious problems facing migrant farm workers today.
*   Students will suggest reforms in existing labor laws that would correct these problems and that will be fair to workers and employers.
*   Students will determine which government officials and legislators would be most helpful in seeing that changes take place.

Reflection on Service Learning: After completing any of the activities above, students should take time to reflect and write their feelings on what the goals of the activity were and whether they felt they were successful in accomplishing them. Students should also note any personal feelings and experiences that occurred during the activity.

ASSIGNMENT SHEET

Vocabulary Activities: Vocabulary terms and definitions.

Agricultural Labor Relations Act (ALRA)
Boycott
Strike
Growers Association ("the Association")
Labor Contractors
Locals
Manongs
Protectorate
"U.S. nationals"

Identify:

Agricultural Workers Organizing Committee (AWOC)

Answer the following questions:

1. What role did Filipino farm workers play in the Delano Grape Strike? What was the significance of the Delano Strike?

2. Define the term "*manong*". Using Philip Vera Cruz as an example, what was life like for a "*manong*"?

3. What was the significance of the 1948 asparagus strike?

4. When was the United Farm Workers union organized? List the Filipino Americans who became part of the UFW.

5. What wages and conditions existed in agricultural labor before and after the establishment of the leadership of the UFW?

6. Describe Philip Vera Cruz's role in the UFW.

7. Why did Vera Cruz eventually leave the union?

8. What is the lasting legacy of the Filipino farm workers?

Lesson Title: Lily Chin: The Courage to Speak Out

Grade Level: 11th Grade U.S. History; 12th Grade U.S. Government/Economics

Unit of Study: Contemporary American Society

History-Social Science Standards: 11.10.5;
Language Arts Standards Grade 11 and 12: 2.0 Reading Comprehension (Focus on Informational Materials) 2.1; 2.3; 2.6 Literary Response and Analysis 3.2

Key Concepts: prejudice, discrimination, hate crime, pivotal event, collaboration

Setting the Context:
On June 19, 1982, Vincent Chin was brutally beaten to death. His death is a tragic example of a hate crime and a heartbreaking case of mistaken identity. Vincent was a young Chinese American who was about to get married. His attackers were two autoworkers that blamed the Japanese for the worsening U.S. auto industry and the loss of U.S. auto plant jobs.

What shocked the Asian American community was the verdict in the trial that followed. His two attackers were found guilty not of murder but of manslaughter, a crime for which they were given probation and required to pay a fine of $3,000 and $780 in court costs. The story does not end with the verdict. For this is not the story of Vincent but that of his grieving mother, Lily. Motivated by the unfairness of the verdict, Lily Chin decided to fight for justice for her son.

Mrs. Chin was an unlikely candidate to conduct a legal battle. An immigrant who barely spoke English, Lily Chin displayed rare courage and determination in her search for justice. The resulting five-year legal battle was a wake up call to the Asian Pacific community to fight anti-Asian violence. Mrs. Chin traveled the country raising money to pay the costs involved in bringing about a civil suit. She was an example of what a determined individual is capable of accomplishing. She brought seniors and immigrants — who could identify with her — into the movement.

Though ultimately unsuccessful in her personal search for justice, Lily Chin's experience triggered a major rethinking within the highly diverse and historically divided Asian Pacific American communities. Chin's experience led to the creation of a number of pan-Asian Pacific American organizations devoted to civil rights and to tracking and combating hate crimes. This lesson focuses on Lily Chin's courage and determination against strong odds.

Expected Learning Outcomes: Students will be able to:

- Describe the anti-Asian bias dramatized in the Vincent Chin murder case.
- Define hate crime.
- Explain the significance of Lily Chin's efforts to the pan-Asian movement.
- Describe the strategies used by Lily Chin and her supporters to gain justice.

Procedure

Guided Instruction:
Introduce this lesson by showing a photo of Vincent Chin. Write the year 1982 and Detroit. Explain that Vincent Chin was murdered that year in the city of Detroit. Note that the 1980s were a time of great uncertainty in the American automotive industry. The Big Three — GM, Ford and Chrysler — were facing stiff competition from Japanese cars and many American automotive workers were losing their jobs. Two angry unemployed auto workers took their anger out on Vincent. But they made a mistake… Vincent was Chinese American. Beaten by a baseball bat, Vincent died of his injuries. Vincent was the only son of Lily Chin. He was 27 years old and just about to get married. This is a story about a grieving mother and her desire to seek justice for her son. Read the chapter.

Review Vocabulary: Review reading and identify terms that students may need to define or have explained. (See Activities for suggested terms). Augment as necessary.

Upon completion of the reading have students complete questions. Review their answers.

Assessment: Conduct a class discussion.

Extension Activities: Students may research the following:

1. The status of organizations created to combat hate crimes in the wake of the death and verdict in the trial of Ronald Ebens and Michael Nitz.
2. List the current hate crime issues by checking websites such as:
- **Statistics on Hate Crimes** The California Attorney General's Criminal Justice Statistics Center compiles annual reports with hate crimes statistics. The publications, entitled "Hate Crime in California," contain data on the number of hate crime victims, the type of incidents experienced by victims, prosecution rates, etc. Website: *http://ag.ca.gov/cjsc/pubs.htm*
- **The National Asian Pacific American Legal Consortium (NAPALC)** compiles annual reports, entitled "Audit of Violence Against Asian Pacific Americans." These reports profile hate crime incidents and provide data on their prevalence in the Asian and Pacific American community nationally. Website: *http://www.napalc.org/dcm.asp?id=50*
- **The Local Law Enforcement Hate Crimes Prevention Act** Explanation of provisions of the Local Law Enforcement Hate Crimes Prevention Act *http://www.civilrights.org/assets/pdfs/HRC-LLEHCPA-One-Pager1-23-07.pdf*

Service Learning: Students can develop projects such as:

- Posters and public address announcement to educate their classmates on the nature and harms of hate crimes and how to report a hate crime. One source of information: *Reporting a Hate Crime.* The National Asian Pacific American Legal Consortium (NAPALC) has developed a Hate Crimes Community Toolkit that provides resources for community members to report a hate crime, work with law enforcement, and secure assistance for victims. Website: *http://www.napalc.org/dcm.asp?id=50*
- See 101 Ways to Combat Prejudice *http://www.adl.org/prejudice/default.asp*
- Letter writing campaign to lobby for passage of comprehensive hate crime legislation
- Compilation of local hate crime prevention resources

Reflection on Service Learning:
After completing any of the activities above, students should take time to reflect and write their feelings on what the goals of the activity were and whether they felt they were successful in accomplishing them. Students should also note any personal feelings and experiences that occurred during the activity.

VINCENT CHIN

Activities

Vocabulary: Explain the following terms

Hate crime
Stereotypes
Civil rights
Pan-Asian movement

Focus Questions:

1. Who was Vincent Chin? Describe the circumstances around his death.

2. What was the charge and the verdict in the trial of Vincent's killers?

3. Describe Lily Chin, Vincent's mother. What did she decide to do when she heard the verdict?

4. Why did some people call Lily Chin, the "Rosa Parks of Asian Americans"?

5. How did Asian American communities react to the verdict?

6. What did Lily Chin's experiences teach the Asian Pacific American communities? What lessons can be learned today?

Lesson Title: A Family Educates to Prevent Hate Crimes: The Case of Joseph Ileto

Grade Level: 11th Grade U.S. History; 12th Grade U.S. Government/Economics

Unit of Study: Contemporary American Society

History-Social Science Standards: 11.11.7.

Key Concepts: prejudice, discrimination, hate crime, media invisibility

Setting the Context:
Students need to be aware of the tragic consequences of hate crimes — violent acts against people, property or organizations solely because of the group to which they belong or with which they are identified. Two compelling examples exist within the Asian Pacific community. What is particularly unique is the response of family members who refused to grieve in silence.

The hate crime killing of Vincent Chin in 1982 activated his mother to demand justice for her son. On August 10, 1999 another hate crime occurred that shook the Asian Pacific American community… this time the crime occurred in California and the victim was Joseph Ileto, a Filipino American mail carrier who was murdered, killed by a self-professed white supremacist, Buford O. Furrow, Joseph Ileto's death was overshadowed by the shooting spree committed by Furrow at a Jewish community center earlier that same day. Children and adults were wounded at the North Valley Jewish Community Center during the incident, luckily no one died.

The death of their beloved Joseph was a senseless act, and the Ileto family decided to act rather than mourn in silence. In the years following Joseph's death, his family (mother Lilian, brother and sister-in-law, Ismael and Deena, and sisters Carmina and Raquel) have become vocal advocates for stronger federal hate crimes legislation. They have participated in marches and rallies, and addressed city council meetings and other forums. Their response to the death of Joseph serves as an example of what ordinary people can do.

Expected Learning Outcomes: Students will be able to:

*   Define hate crime.
*   List the identifiable social groups that are targets of hate crimes.
*   Explain the importance of balanced media coverage of hate crimes.
*   Describe the efforts of the Ileto family to fight hate crimes.
*   Describe the rationale for the passage of strong federal hate crime laws.

Procedure

Guided Instruction: Introduce this lesson with the Albert Einstein quote: *"The world is a dangerous place to live in, not because of the people that are evil, but because of the people who won't do anything about it."* Explain that this lesson highlights the efforts of an ordinary family that had to face the unthinkable — the hate crime murder of a beloved son and brother by a white supremacist. When they lost Joseph, the Ileto family did something. Introduce the reading and ask students to find out what motivated the Ileto family to become involved in the fight against hate.

Assessment: Upon completion of the reading, students will complete questions.

Extension Activities: Students may research the following:

*   Nature of hate crime *http://lahumanrelations.org/hatecrime/hatecrimereport.htm*
*   School activities to reduce hate motivated incidents and hate crimes on campus and in the community.
*   Local organizations that fight against hate such as the Asian Pacific American Legal Center, Los An-

geles Human Relations Commission and national organizations such as the Anti-Defamation League, Southern Poverty Law Center.

- *Local Law Enforcement Hate Crimes Prevention Act (LLEHCPA)* introduced in 2007. Examine the current status of hate crime legislation.

Service Learning: Students can develop projects such as:

- Posters and public address announcement to educate their classmates on the nature and harms of hate crimes and how to report a hate crime. One source of information: *Reporting a Hate Crime.* The National Asian Pacific American Legal Consortium (NAPALC) has developed a Hate Crimes Community Toolkit that provides resources for community members to report a hate crime, work with law enforcement, and secure assistance for victims. Website: *www.napalc.org/*

- See 101 Ways to Combat Prejudice *http://www.adl.org/prejudice/default.asp*
- Letter writing campaign to lobby for passage of comprehensive hate crime legislation.
- Compilation of local hate crime prevention resources.

Reflection on Service Learning:
After completing any of the activities above, students should take time to reflect and write their feelings on what the goals of the activity were and whether they felt they were successful in accomplishing them. Students should also note any personal feelings and experiences that occurred during the activity.

Activities

Explain the following terms:

Hate crime
Racial discrimination
Model minority
Media invisibility
Social activism
Multicultural coalition
Bayanihan

Answer the following questions:

1. Who was Joseph Ileto? Why was he killed?

2. What was the penalty given to Buford O. Furrow, the murderer of Joseph Ileto?

3. How did the media treat the death of Joseph and the shooting at the North Valley Jewish Center?

4. How did the actions of the media affect the Ileto family?

5. Two other brutal hate crimes occurred during the same time period of Joseph's death. How did these crimes affect the Ileto family?

6. What role did Ismael Ileto assume after Joseph's murder?

7. What is the message of the Ileto family to others?

Lesson Title: Breaking the Color Line in Hollywood: Beulah Ong Kwoh, Actor

Grade Level: 11 U.S. History

Unit of Study: Contemporary American Society

California History-Social Science Standards: U.S. History 11.11.6.
California Language Arts Standards 3.0 Literary Response and Analysis 3.2
Listening and Speaking Strategies Comprehension 1.1; 1.2 1.3

Key Concepts:
Diversity, identity, stereotypes, change, community service, perspective

Setting the Context:
American media has long neglected to depict the lives of people of color. Only in recent years has there been a presence of people of color in films. It has taken the effort of many unsung heroes to increase the representation of people of color in the media.

Highlighting the experiences of Beulah Kwoh (Quo) provides insights into this experience. Early roles depicting people of color were often played by white actors in make-up. Most of the roles were stereotypical in nature. When roles were finally given to people of color, they continued the stereotypical portrayals. There has been a long and continuing struggle to gain visibility and realistic depiction.

As a pioneering actor of color, Beulah Kwoh faced the challenges and worked to change the limiting constraints imposed. Her talent, dedication and commitment to others left a lasting legacy within the Asian American acting community. Her experience as an Asian American actor provides insights faced by other actors of color. The depiction of any group influences the way the group is perceived and treated in the broader society.

Expected Learning Outcomes: Students will be able to:

*   Describe the barriers that Beulah Kwoh as an Asian American had to overcome.
*   Describe the various strategies she used to gain positive roles.
*   Assess whether the same barriers exist for other actors of color.
*   Evaluate the present opportunities afforded to Asian American, African American, Latino actors.

Procedure

Guided Instruction:

Use a series of stereotypical ethnic images found in the media. Ask students why they should be concerned about the use of such images. Seek definition for the word "stereotype." Elicit additional examples of media stereotypes. Explain that for many people, the media informs their views and attitudes of groups they do not know. Ask for examples.

Set up two columns on the board or overhead. Label first column — Stereotypical Image. Label second column — Message conveyed by image.

Write the term "media invisibility." Explain that since the early days of motion pictures and television, people of color were rarely seen. The struggle to gain visibility, a place in entertainment media is the topic of today's lesson.

Provide clarification for some of the terms in the reading such as: Phi Beta Kappa — an honorary society, founded in 1776, of college students and graduates whose members are chosen on the basis of high academic standing.

Assessment: Upon finishing the reading, students will complete reading questions and short quiz. Students may also conduct a survey of either current films or television programs and identify ethnic individuals featured and the roles they played. Evaluate if the portrayal was positive or negative.

Extension Activities: Students may research ethnic stereotypes in the American media. Possible sites include:

Teaching Tolerance *www.tolerance.org*
Children Now, Advocacy Group examining role of the media in children's lives
MANAA: Media Action Network for Asian Americans *http://www.manaa.org/*
YAAMS: Young African Americans against Media Stereotypes *http://www.yaaams.org/index-n8.php*

Service Learning: Los Angeles Unified School District has a series of suggested Service Learning Projects at the following website: *http://notebook.lausd.net/portal/page?_pageid=33,179449&_dad=ptl&_schema=PTL_EP*
Create a project related to film or television media literacy.

Reflection on Service Learning: After completing any of the activities above, students should take time to reflect and write their feelings on what the goals of the activity were and whether they felt they were successful in accomplishing them. Students should also note any personal feelings and experiences that occurred during the activity.

Activities

Vocabulary: There are a number of terms unique to the entertainment industry. Define the following:

Color line
Dialect coach
Greasepaint
Character roles
Director
Producer
Playwright
Cinematographer
Story rights

Identify:

East West Players
Association of Asian Pacific American Artists (AAPAA)
Angel Island
Media invisibility
Stereotype

Questions:

1. Select three adjectives to describe Beulah's family and early life. Explain the reasons for your choice of adjectives.

2. Why was it important for Beulah to have the support of her husband in her choice of an acting career?

3. Why did Beulah chose to attend the Desilu Workshop?

4. What was the reason for the creation of the East West Players?

5. Aside from her acting talents, what other strengths did Beulah contribute to the East West Players?

6. List some of the stereotypical roles that Asian actors portrayed. Why is this objectionable?

7. As a pioneer in television, Beulah Kwoh earned several "firsts." Identify and describe their significance.

8. How did Beulah Kwoh help pave the way for other actors of color? What lessons can we learn from her experiences?

Lesson Title: Building Bridges between Races: Kyung Won Lee, Investigative Journalist

Grade Level: 11th Grade U.S. History; 12th Grade U.S. Government

Unit of Study: Contemporary American Society

History Social Science Standards: Grade 11 U.S. History 11.10.5, 11.11.1, 11.11.6, 11.11.7
Grade 12 U.S. Government 12.8.1, 12.8.2

Language Arts Standards Grade 11 and 12
2.1 Reading Comprehension (Focus on Informational Materials) 3.2, 3.8
Writing 2.4 Write historical investigation reports a.b.c.
1.0 Listening and Speaking Strategies 1.1, 1.2, 1.3
2.0 Speaking Applications (Genres and Their Characteristics) 2.2 a. b. c. d.

Key Concepts:
Interactions, Color-line, Racism, Conflict, Coalition Building, Pivotal Event

Setting the Context:
Korean Americans are one of the fastest-growing ethnic communities in the United States. The Korean immigrant experience in the U.S. can be traced back one hundred years. However, Korean immigration increased significantly only following the passage of the Immigration and Naturalization Act of 1965. The life and work of K.W. (short for Kyung Won) Lee, a pioneering Asian American journalist, illustrates the common hardships and the unique challenges faced by Korean Americans. Among his peers, K.W. Lee is considered "the dean of Asian American journalism." Throughout his journalistic career, he used the print media to create public awareness of the many injustices suffered by the poor and/or immigrant communities and to build bridges between the races. His personal story and his actions exemplify an individual who understand the fact that "no man is an island" and whose efforts have consistently supported expanded communication and understanding between races.

Expected Learning Outcomes: Students will be able to:

• Describe the journalistic career of K.W. Lee.
• Illustrate the "bridge-building" steps employed by K.W. Lee to create better understanding.
• Define stereotype and scapegoat and describe their negative impact on society.

Procedure

Guided Instruction
Introduce this lesson by sharing several photos of the 1992 L.A. Rebellion/Riot or a newspaper front page covering the event. Ask students what they know about the event. Based on the students' response, provide needed background.

Background information: Catalyst: Acquittal of the four white Los Angeles Police Department (LAPD) officers in the beating of a black motorist, Rodney King. The outrage over the decision led to the city erupting into flames and chaos.

When: Six days – April 29 to May 4, 1992
Areas affected: South-Central Los Angeles, Koreatown, Hollywood, Mid-Wilshire, Watts and Westwood as well as Beverly Hills, Compton, Culver City, Hawthorne, Long Beach, Norwalk and Pomona.

What happened: People looted stores, set fire to buildings, and destroyed sections of the city. Fifty-eight people died, neighborhoods were left in ruins, and the damage was estimated at over a billion dollars.

Hardest hit: Korean small-business owners who owned shops in South Central L.A. and neighboring Koreatown. Some 2,000 Korean-owned businesses were completely destroyed in the riots and an estimated $400 million dollars of damage was done. A 1994 survey revealed that one-third of Korean-owned businesses in the area were never rebuilt. Many Koreans moved out of L.A. altogether, or moved south to Orange County.

Introduce K.W. Lee, considered the first Asian immigrant to work for mainstream newspapers in the continental United States. List the issues he has covered: 1) civil rights struggles in the South in the early 1960s, 2) massive vote buying practices in southern West Virginia and 3) the plight of Appalachian coal miners — Note these are not Asian issues.

Assign the reading, have students identify other issues covered by Lee. Have students identify his efforts to create awareness of the Korean American community and increase understanding between the diverse communities in which he worked.

Assessment: Discuss the reading. Have students respond to the questions. Encourage comments and observations. Ask for clarification, elaboration, explanation and record the main ideas discussed. Summarize the points of the discussion.

Extension Activities: Students may conduct research on the following on the internet for more information on:
K.W. Lee by accessing the UC Davis University Library Digital Project

1974 Chol Soo Lee murder case. The movie *True Believer*, starring James Woods playing a defense attorney was based on the Chol Soo Lee case. The movie failed to recognize the investigative reporting (five year-long coverage, 120 articles) that was pivotal to a new trial and eventual acquittal of Chol Soo Lee. His role was invisible to Hollywood. Review *True Believer* and write a film critique based on the true facts of the case.

1992 Los Angeles Riot — Impact on the Korean American Community

Service Learning:
Suggested project: Identify individuals at school or in the local community who are positive role models and bridge builders. Develop a campaign to appropriately recognize them.

Reflection on Service Learning:
After completing any of the activities above, students should take time to reflect and write their feelings on what the goals of the activity were and whether they felt they were successful in accomplishing them. Students should also note any personal feelings and experiences that occurred during the activity.

Activities

Vocabulary: Explain the following terms

| Color-line | Stereotypes | Civil rights | pan-Asian movement | icon |

Identify:

| Appalachia | Chol Soo Lee case | 1.5 generation |

Focus Questions:

1. Who was K.W. Lee? When did he immigrate to the United States?

2. Where did he first report about discrimination in the U.S.?

3. What are some common Korean stereotypes?

4. What triggered the 1992 Los Angeles Riot? How did the riot impact the Korean American community?

5. What specific actions did K.W. Lee take as a journalist to counter those stereotypes and build greater understanding?

Lesson Title: One Man Seeks Justice from a Nation: Korematsu v. United States

Grade Level: 11th Grade; 12th Grade U.S. Government

Unit of Study: Post-World War II America (1945-1960), Continuity and Change

History-Social Science Standards: 11.7.5
U.S. Government Standards: 12.5.1 12.6

Key Concepts: Equality, Discrimination, Civil Rights, military necessity, racism

Setting the Context:
During World War II, Americans of Japanese ancestry and their immigrant parents were removed from their homes in the Western states by Executive Order 9066 signed by President Franklin D. Roosevelt. The explanation given was "military necessity." The overwhelming majority of Japanese Americans reacted to the internment by complying with the government's order, hoping to prove their loyalty as Americans.

A few chose to defy the order. Fred Korematsu, a young welder was one of those few. Korematsu was later arrested and was transferred to Topaz, Utah, one of the ten War Relocation Authority camps. He later challenged the government. His case went to the Supreme Court. Most history books discuss the Korematsu decision but end with the Supreme Court upholding the constitutionality of the decision. It is important that students learn why the Korematsu decision was revisited in 1984 and why the judge sided with Korematsu.

Fear drove Americans to accept the rationale of "military necessity" without questions even though American citizens were to be incarcerated and denied their civil rights. Since the terrorist attacks of 9/11, the American public face similar concerns over safety. The delicate balance between civil liberties and national security are again issues of concern. Reading about Fred Korematsu may help students to understand how the lives of average Americans can be affected when fear overcomes reason.

Expected Learning Outcomes: Students will be able to:

*   Identify the rights of U.S. citizens protected by the Constitution and the Bill of Rights.
*   Describe the stresses imposed on the delicate balance between civil liberties and security in times of crisis.
*   Evaluate how the government not only protects but can also limit individual rights.
*   Analyze the consequences of taking unpopular stands.
*   Identify the constitutional issues raised by the experiences of Fred Korematsu.

Procedure

Guided Instruction: Introduce the reading with a mock-up of the exclusion order. Conduct a guided discussion of the key events covered in the reading. Briefly describe the life of Fred Korematsu before the beginning of U.S. involvement in WWII.

Assessment:
Students will be assessed based on completion of written assignment.

Extension Activities: Students may research the following on the internet:

Street Law & The Supreme Court Historical Society Presents… Landmark Cases of the Supreme Court
http://www.landmarkcases.org/korematsu/home.html
Extensive information and activities about the Korematsu case. Contains a section that makes the connection to current cases involving *Rasul v. Bush* and *Al Odah v. United States*, detainees at Guantanamo Bay, Cuba, and Jose Padilla, an American citizen. Respond to the question: Do you think terrorism fears can escalate and result in another internment of innocent Americans? Why or why not?
Asian American Bar Association of the Greater Bay Area

http://www.aaba-bay.com/aaba/showpage.asp?code=korematsucase
Detailed information specific to the Korematsu case

Expand research to Gordon Hirabayashi and Minoru Yasui, who also challenged the curfew and detention and whose cases also went to the Supreme Court. For more information about them, go to:
Discover Nikkei* Japanese Migrants and Their Descendants
http://www.discovernikkei.org/wiki/index.php/Resistance

Smithsonian National Museum of American History — A More Perfect Union Court Cases
http://americanhistory.si.edu/perfectunion/non-flash/justice_court.html

Densho Website:
http://www.densho.org/learning/default.asp
Site dedicated to preserving the World War II experiences of Japanese Americans. Site contains historical information, firsthand accounts, and lessons about the incarceration.

Sources:
Chin, Steven A. *When Justice Failed: The Fred Korematsu Story*. Steck-Vaughn Company: New York, 1993
Irons, Peter. *Justice at War*. Oxford University Press: New York, 1983

Service Learning:
Suggested projects: Have students research the plight of Latin American Japanese removed from their homes, incarcerated in the U.S during WWII and lobby for justice and equitable compensation. Go to Campaign for Justice website at *http://www.campaignforjusticejla.org/*

Reflection on Service Learning: After completing any of the activities above, students should take time to reflect and write their feelings on what the goals of the activity were and whether they felt they were successful in accomplishing them. Students should also note any personal feelings and experiences that occurred during the activity.

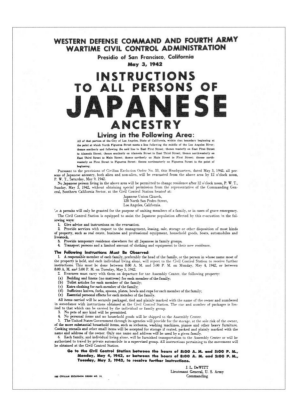

COPY OF EXCLUSION POSTER

Writ of error *coram nobis*
Pro bono
Nullification of conviction
Vacated decision

Identify the following persons:

Ernest Besig
Peter Irons
Aiko Herzig-Yoshinaga
Gordon Hirabayashi
Minoru Yasui
Dale Minami
Judge Marilyn Patel

Describe the importance of the following:

Executive Order 9066
Assembly Centers
Internment/Concentration camps
American Civil Liberties Union (ACLU)
Japanese American Citizens League (JACL)
Racial profiling
Civil Liberties Act of 1988

Answer the following questions:

1. Describe Fred Korematsu's background.

2. In what ways did Fred Korematsu experience discrimination prior to the issuance of Executive Order 9066?

3. What did Executive Order 9066 authorize?

4. What did Fred Korematsu do when ordered to report to Tanforan Assembly Center?

5. What role did Ernest Besig play in Korematsu's life?

6. What was the decision of the Supreme Court in the *Korematsu vs. U.S.* case in 1944?

7. What happened in 1983 that allowed Fred to challenge the 1944 Supreme Court decision?

8. What important discovery did Peter Irons and Aiko Herzig-Yoshinaga make?

9. What did the young lawyers hope to accomplish by taking on the Korematsu case?

10. What was Judge Marilyn Patel's verdict in the new trial?

What do you think?

Why do you think Japanese American citizens were interned while citizens of Italian and German descent were not?

Explain the connection between the *coram nobis* cases and the government apology and monetary payments to surviving internees?

Japanese Americans were the object of racial profiling during WWII. Has racial profiling increased since 9/11? Should you be concerned? Why or why not?

Lesson Title: American Veteran in Exile: Manong Faustino "Peping" Baclig

Grade Level: 11th Grade

Unit of Study: Grade 11: World War II and Its Consequences, Post-World War II America (1945-1960), Continuity and Change; Grade 12: Principals of a Civil Society

California History-Social Science Standards: 11.7.5
California U.S. Government Standards: 12.5.1

Key Concepts: Justice, Fairness, Redress, Self-determination

Setting the Context:
December 7, 1941 is highlighted in U.S. history books because it is the date Japan attacked Pearl Harbor, Hawaii, bringing the U.S. into World War II. Most students, however, are unaware that the attack on Pearl Harbor was only one part of Japan's invasion plans. The Japanese also attacked three other Pacific locations: the U.S. Army's Far East Air Force at Clark Field in the Philippines, British Hong Kong, and British Malaya. Over the next few months the Japanese Army marched through Southeast Asia, and by March 1942 the Japanese controlled almost 500 million people and four million square miles of land. It was only in the Philippines that the Japanese experienced strong resistance.

Filipino Soldiers of WWII
The role of Filipino solders in the Philippines is a little known story. President Roosevelt used an executive order to recruit Filipinos in the war. Filipino recruits recited the following pledge:

"I, __[Name]__, do solemnly swear...that I will bear true faith and allegiance...to the United States of America...that I will serve them honestly and faithfully...against all their enemies whomsoever...and I will obey the orders...of the President of the United States...And the orders of the officers appointed over me...according to the rules and Articles of War."

With this pledge, approximately 250,000 Filipino men joined the U.S. Armed Forces in the months before and the days just after the Japanese attack on Pearl Harbor. There were several different categories of Filipino troops that became involved at different points in time: 1) Regular Philippine Scouts (old Scouts) 2) Commonwealth Army of the Philippines and the Philippine Army 3) Special Philippine Scouts (New Scouts) 4) Recognized Guerilla units.

For the next several years, they would share the fate of their American counterparts on the battlefield, in prisoner of war camps, and throughout the countryside as part of the guerrilla resistance. Accordingly, Washington promised them the same health and pension benefits as their American brothers. Even after the war, in October 1945, Gen. Omar Bradley, then administrator of the Veterans Administration, reaffirmed that they were to be treated like any other American veterans.

Benefits Denied
Despite promises made, on February 18, 1946, Congress passed and President Harry Truman signed the Rescission Act of 1946. It said that the service of Filipinos "shall not be deemed to be or to have been service in the military or national forces of the United States or any component thereof or any law of the United States conferring rights, privileges or benefits."

This reading presents the story of the WWII Filipino veterans and their long struggle for fairness and justice through the experiences of one Filipino veteran, Faustino "Peping" Baclig.

Expected Learning Outcomes: Students will be able to:

- Describe the relationship of the U.S. to the Philippines.
- Identify the role of Filipino soldiers in World War II.

- Describe the treatment of WWII prisoners of war in the Philippines (Bataan Death March).
- Explain the U.S. promise made to Filipino soldiers.
- Identify the strategies used by the Filipino veterans to seek redress.

Procedure

Guided Instruction:
Write December 7, 1941 on the board. Ask students to explain the significance of the date. Students should respond with the attack on Pearl Harbor. Write Hong Kong, Malaya and Philippines on the board. Explain that Japan also attacked these locations on Dec. 7. Explain that in 1898, the Philippines became a territory of the United States and in 1941 the Philippines was in a 10-year transition period towards independence. The government was in Filipino control but the military remained in U.S. control. Show a map of the Pacific area — preferably a map of the Pacific Rim. Name the countries conquered by Japan — emphasize the valiant resistance of forces in the Philippines.

Explain that today's lesson highlights the experiences of Filipino soldiers who were "drafted" by President Roosevelt and who fought side by side with American troops in the Philippines. (Show poster of Fighting Filipinos). Introduce Manong Peping Baclig and have students read his story.

Enrichment: Students may research the following on the internet:

An American Experience — Bataan Rescue *http://www.pbs.org/wgbh/amex/bataan/index.html*
People and Events: Filipinos and the World. *http://www.pbs.org/wgbh/amex/bataan/peopleevents/p_filipinos.html*
Map of the Philippines *http://www.pbs.org/wgbh/amex/bataan/sfeature/sf_map.html*

Assessment:
Students will be assessed based on completion of one of the following:
Multiple choice quiz
Short paper on one of the following topics:
- The Untold Story of Filipino Soldiers Fighting for the U.S. in WWII.
- The Fight of WWII Filipino Veterans for Justice and Equity.

Source of poster: Fighting Filipinos
http://www.artsnotdead.com/Fighting-Filipinos-world-war-ii-US-military-poster-p/
prop_usa_filipinos.htm

Suggested projects:
Students write letters of support to members of the House of Representatives.
Students develop a Powerpoint presentation for other classes to secure support for veterans.

Reflection on Service Learning:
After completing any of the activities above, students should take time to reflect and write their feelings on what the goals of the activity were and whether they felt they were successful in accomplishing them. Students should also note any personal feelings and experiences that occurred during the activity.

Activities

Vocabulary: Explain the following terms.

Manong
Guerrilla
Posthumous

Identify:

U.S. Army Forces in the Far East (USAFFE)
Gen. Douglas MacArthur
Bataan Death March
Rescission Act of 1946
American Coalition for Filipino Veterans (ACFV)

Answer the following questions:

1. How many Filipino soldiers fought in the U.S. Army Forces in the Far East (USAFFE)?

2. What was the status of the Philippines in 1941?

3. Why was the resistance offered by the USAFFE so important to the U.S. war effort in the Pacific?

4. Describe the treatment of Manong "Peping" and the other American and Filipino prisoners of war (POWs) after the fall of Corregidor and Bataan.

5. Why did Congress pass the Rescission Act of 1946? Why did Filipino veterans feel that this was a grave injustice?

6. Describe the strategies used by Manong "Peping" and other Filipino veterans in their quest for justice.

Think About It

It is now more than 60 years since the end of World War II. Should the United States honor its promise to Manong "Peping" and the other Filipino veterans? Explain your answer.

Lesson Title: Who Took the Rap? A Call to Action

Grade Level: 11th Grade U.S. History; 12th Grade U.S. Government/Economics

Unit of Study: Contemporary American Society

History-Social Science Standards: 11.11.7.

Key Concepts: civil rights, terrorism, scapegoating, discrimination, racial profiling

Setting the Context:
The attacks on the World Trade Center and the Pentagon on 9/11 changed life in the United States. Emotions ran the gamut from grief, anger, revenge and disbelief. One of the most dramatic changes was one of attitude. Since 9/11 the attitude of the general public towards brown-skinned people of Arab, Asian or even Latino descent has grown increasingly intolerant. Suspicion, distrust and hate were directed against these groups.

Fear has driven people to relinquish precious civil rights in the name of national security. Students need to be reminded that it is in such times of crisis that democracy is most threatened.

The readings provided in *Untold Civil Rights Stories* identifies a number of areas that continue to offer civil rights challenges. The individuals identified in our chapters have waged a valiant fight but the struggles continue. In *Who Took the Rap? A Call to Action*, young people are invited to lend energies and voices to service learning projects that would benefit their communities.

Service Learning:
Service learning projects are based on identified needs of local communities. Suggested projects include:

- Heighten awareness of the harms of hate crimes. Victims of discrimination are often not aware of the laws that protect them. Students and their parents can be targets of discrimination — service learning projects can involve the need to be aware of the protections existing laws provide and to lobby for the expansion of the level of protection.
- Recognition of the poor working conditions and wages for migrant workers and garment workers. Many students come from families in which relatives have or continue to work in fields or factories. Service learning projects to educate others of the problems and to work for legislative action.
- Introduction to the role of local activists in the civil rights movement. The inspiring story of members of their own community would teach students that great movements involve regular people standing up for a just cause. Write articles, produce media to educate others.
- Focus on religious minorities in the U.S. who have few advocates. They are victims of persecution, and their plight often go unnoticed. Students can become advocates for such groups. This also allows students to have a deeper respect for the religious freedoms that exist in the United States.
- Recognition of the influence of media. Monitor the media to evaluate the balance of coverage. Contact media sources that demonstrate bias and demand more balanced news or representation in media productions.

Reflection on Service Learning:
After completing any of the activities above, students should take time to reflect and write their feelings on what the goals of the activity were and whether they felt they were successful in accomplishing them. Students should also note any personal feelings and experiences that occurred during the activity.

Lesson Title: Defending the Unpopular Immigrant

Grade Level: 11th Grade U.S. History; 12th Grade U.S. Government/Economics

Unit of Study: Contemporary American Society

History-Social Science Standards: 11.11.1.

Key Concepts: Immigration, controversy, multiple perspectives, undocumented immigrants

Setting the Context: This lesson covers an issue that arouses a great deal of passion — immigrants. The fear of terrorism now colors the immigration debate, with undocumented workers and their families at the center of the discussion. Barriers have been built to prevent the arrival of new undocumented individuals and the push to deport those already here has increased. This lesson focuses on the immigration policies and laws that affect undocumented immigrants and legal residents ("green card" holders) who have been convicted of crimes.

Bill Ong Hing, civil rights attorney and law professor, represents those who are going through the deportation process — an unpopular and difficult task. He provides a very human insight into their plight. He provides insights into the complexity of this issue through specific experiences of individuals and families: Felipe Cabral family (Mexico), John Suey (China), and Many Uch (Cambodia). To make sound decisions, it is critical for students to have a full understanding of the issues, especially the impact on the lives of real people.

Expected Learning Outcomes: Students will be able to:

*   Cite the arguments for and against the presence of undocumented immigrants in the U.S.
*   Describe the conditions in the home country of undocumented immigrants/ refugees.
*   Explain the legal problems faced by undocumented immigrants and/or immigrants who hold a green card.

Procedure

Guided Instruction: Write the word "Controversy" on the board or overhead. List several issues that provoke strong disagreements or feelings, ending with the word "Immigrants." Note that since the terrorist attacks on September 11, 2001 anti-immigrant attitudes have increased and concerns about undocumented or illegal immigrants have intensified.

Explain that the reading presents a unique perspective on this issue. Introduce Bill Ong Hing, professor of law at the University of California Davis. Explain that throughout his long career, he has worked for the "underdogs" of society.

In this chapter, Professor Hing gives students not statistics nor government policies, but the very personal stories of his clients. Note that three different families are described in the chapter, the Felipe Cabral family, John Suey and Many Uch. Explain that this lesson is intended to provide additional information on the highly volatile and complex issue of immigration. He gives students a clear understanding of his point of view by using the word "undocumented" rather than the word "illegal."

Extension Activities
The passage of the Immigration Act of 1996 expanded the definition of aggravated felonies. Find out what this means to undocumented and green card immigrants.

Service Learning: Los Angeles Unified School District Service Learning Projects
Go to *http://notebook.lausd.net/portal/page?_pageid=33,179449&_dad=ptl&_schema=PTL_EP*

Assessment: Compare and contrast the three persons in the reading. Review the following facts.

Who	Country of Origin	Reasons for leaving home country	Mode of entry into U.S.	Original Immigration Status	Relevant Immigration Policy
Cabral family					
John Suey					
Many Uch					

Students assume the role of immigration judge. Explain that each of the defendants have appeared in his/her court seeking a second chance. Decide on the fate of each, explain in detail why the defendant was given or denied a second chance.

Students may research the following:

"Monitoring the Media" – examines bias in the media. Media influences the public's perception of illegal or undocumented immigrants. Survey news outlets (print, radio, television or the internet). Identify the connotation of descriptive terms used to describe immigrants. Identify words with positive connotations and those with negative connotations. Tally the use of words. Explain how do these words influence public attitudes.

"Making Your Opinion Count: Influencing Immigration Policy" – Students will use the current debate in Congress over changes in immigration policy to explore ways they can influence the decisions that are made.

Teach In on Immigration – Students will research immigration history, significant legislation affecting immigrants, current proposals for changes and what individuals can do to influence decisions.

Reflection on Service Learning:
After completing any of the activities above, students should take time to reflect and write their feelings on what the goals of the activity were and whether they felt they were successful in accomplishing them. Students should also note any personal feelings and experiences that occurred during the activity.

Activities

Vocabulary: Explain the following terms

La migra
Green Card holders
Amnesty
Deportation
Repatriation

Identify:

1986 Immigration Reform Control Act
Policy client
Aggravated felony

Comprehension Questions:

1. When did the Cabral family enter the United States? Why was the family arrested?

2. How was the Cabral family able to finally secure legal status?

3. How did John Suey and his family enter the United States?

4. List the factors that you feel contributed the most to John Suey's criminal behavior.

5. What factors finally enabled John Suey to turn his life around for the better?

6. What circumstances allowed the immigration authorities to arrest and begin deportation proceedings against John Suey? How was John Suey able to win his fight to stay in the U.S.?

7. How did Many Uch's background differ from John Suey? How were John and Many similar?

8. What is the difference between entering the U.S. as an immigrant or a refugee?

9. What were the changes in immigration law in 1996 that affected Many Uch?

10. How will the Repatriation Agreement between the U.S. and Cambodia affect Many Uch?

Think About It

Bill Ong Hing made the statement:

"We have the power to exclude, to punish and to criminalize these border crossers. But that power must be implemented morally and ethically with an understanding that we are dealing with real human beings."

What are your thoughts about the treatment of people like the Cabrals, John Suey and Many Uch?

Lesson Title: A Citizen Fights for His Civil Rights after 9/11: Amric Singh Rathour

Grade Level: 11th Grade U.S. History; 12th Grade U.S. Government/Economics

Unit of Study: Contemporary American Society

Standards: History-Social Science 11.10.5, 11.11.7; U.S. Government 12.10

Key Concepts: freedom of religion, discrimination, perception, civil rights, coalition

Setting the Context:
Religious liberty was central to the Founders' vision for America, and is the "first freedom" listed in the First Amendment of the Bill of Rights. A critical component of religious liberty is the right of people of all faiths to participate fully in the benefits and privileges of society without facing discrimination based on their religion. This is a statement from the Department of Justice. However, instances of discrimination do occur. The experiences of Amric Singh Rathour described in this reading will introduce students to the Sikhs and their distinct religion and his personal fight against religious discrimination in the workplace.

Students will learn that of the twenty-four million Sikhs worldwide, there are an estimated 500,000 Sikhs in the United States. Sikhism is the fifth largest religion in the world, tracing its origin to Punjab, located in present-day Pakistan and northern India. In the post-9/11 era American Sikhs have found themselves mistaken for Muslims because men wear turbans as part of their religious practices. As a result they have faced physical violence as well as discrimination.

Amric Singh Rathour, an American-born Sikh, wanted to be a police officer. He, like all observant Sikh men, wore a turban and had a beard. He completed basic training and was abruptly fired because of his turban. This reading chronicles Rathour's decision to fight to retain his job.

Expected Learning Outcomes: Students will be able to:

•   Describe the basic practices of the Sikh religion
•   Explain the basis of the job discrimination action against Amric Singh Rathour
•   Describe the strategies used by Rathour to obtain justice

Procedure

Guided Instruction:
Begin this lesson by sharing several photos of men in various headdresses — include a photo of a Sikh (Amric Singh Rathour's photo provided below). Ask students to identify the background of each man. Most students will assume all the photos are of Arabs or Muslims. Identify the Sikh. Explain that Sikhs are a separate religion with no connections to Islam or Arabs. Explain that after 9/11, there were a number of Sikhs that were mistaken for Arabs and suffered violence…even death in some cases. That is why this chapter is important. It will highlight the Sikhs in America, many have been here for more than 100 years.

This chapter will introduce Amric Singh Rathour, an American-born Sikh. As a member of his faith, he is required to follow five articles of faith. One of which is for Sikh men to wear turbans. Have students find out what happened when he was forced to choose between his desire to be an NYPD officer and a member of his faith. Ask students to read and find out how one man was able to challenge a discriminatory policy of the NYPD and win.

Extension Activities: Students may research the following on the internet:

Jagjit Singh – First Sikh reserve officer in the Los Angeles County Sheriff's Department
Federal Laws protecting religious freedom *http://www.usdoj.gov/crt/religdisc/know_your_rights.pdf]*

Sikh Organizations and their functions: Sikh Council on Religion and Education (SCORE) *http://www.sikh-councilusa.org/page.aspx?tabname=Homes*

Assessment: Upon completion of the reading, have students complete the activities. Conduct a review. Have students orally trace the specific strategies that lead to a successful outcome.

Service Learning: Fight for Religious Freedom Project
While studying the struggle against religious intolerance in United States history, students will research the current plight of various religious minorities. They will focus on religious groups that are currently the victims of religious intolerance, and contact government officials involved. They will seek to eliminate religious persecution against these groups.

Reflection on Service Learning:
After completing any of the activities above, students should take time to reflect and write their feelings on what the goals of the activity were and whether they felt they were successful in accomplishing them. Students should also note any personal feelings and insights gained.

Activities

Vocabulary: Explain the following terms

Religious exemption
Affiliates
Public advocacy

Identify:

Sikhism
Sikh Coalition
Equal Employment Opportunity Commission (EEOC)

Questions

Answer the following:

1. Why were American Sikhs targets of violence after 9/11?

2. Where did Sikhism originate? What are some of the core beliefs of the Sikh religion?

3. Where was Amric Singh Rathour born? What challenges did he face as a boy?

4. Why was he denied a job as a New York police officer?

5. When and why was the Sikh Coalition established?

6. What was the ruling of the Equal Employment Opportunity Commission to Amric's case?

7. List some of the specific strategies used by Amric and the Sikh Coalition to gain greater public support.

8. Why was a federal lawsuit instituted?

9. How long did it take to resolve the issue? What was the result?

Think About It

From the founding of the country, religious freedom has been of concern. The first item mentioned in the Bill of Rights refers to religion. The First Amendment states: "Congress shall make no laws respecting an establishment of religion, or *prohibiting the free exercise thereof...*" [italics added for emphasis].
Why do you think Amric Singh Rathour as a Sikh American was willing to fight the dress code policy of the NYPD? What important lessons can his experiences teach all of us?

AMRIC SINGH RATHOUR

TIMELINE

By Esther Taira

The timeline below is a sampling of the many events that have impacted our lives. The timeline is divided into three columns, *National/International Events, Events in Ethnic America and events described in "Untold Stories."* Events and lives intertwine in a variety of ways. Can you see the connections? You are invited to add events to any of the three columns.

National/International Events	Ethnic America Events	"Untold Civil Rights" Events
1846-48 Mexican War — U.S. gains territory including California and New Mexico.	**1848** Gold is discovered at Sutter's Mill, CA, drawing Chinese immigrants to the state.	
1861-65 U.S. Civil War	**1865** Chinese laborers are hired to work on the Transcontinental Railroad. *People v. Hall*, California Supreme Court — Ruled that the testimony of a Chinese man who witnessed a murder by a white man was inadmissible.	
	1868 First Japanese immigrants are recruited to work in Hawaii as contract laborers.	
	1869 First group of Japanese immigrants arrive in California and establish the Wakamatsu Colony at Gold Hill.	
1882 Congress passes Chinese Exclusion Act, ending immigration from China and barring Chinese from U.S. citizenship.	**1882** Loss of new immigrant Chinese workers results in increased demand for labor, causing an increase in Japanese immigration to Pacific Coast.	
1886 *Yick Wo v. Hopkins*, U.S. Supreme Court, in a unanimous opinion, rules in favor of Yick Wo, holding that, in discriminating against Chinese laundries, San Francisco was in violation of equal protection when it operates to discriminate in a practice against a racial minority.	**1886** In *Yick Wo v. Hopkins* the U.S. Supreme Court rules for Yick Wo, owner of a Chinese laundry, holding that a San Francisco ordinance discriminated against them.	
1898 Spanish American War. The U.S. annexes Hawaii		
1899 Philippines, Guam, and Puerto Rico annexed by U.S.		
		1904 Philip Vera Cruz is born on Christmas Day in the Philippines.
	1906 (November) — The San Francisco School Board removes children of Japanese and others of "Mongoloid" ancestry from regular schools and places them in a segregated school.	
1907 The Gentleman's Agreement is signed between the U.S. and Japan. In this agreement, Japan volunteers to halt labor immigration to the U.S.		
	1909 Angel Island, an immigration facility in San Francisco Bay, opens in order to examine Asian Pacific Islander immigrants upon their arrival to the West Coast.	

TIMELINE

National/International Events		Ethnic America Events		"Untold Civil Rights" Events	
1917	U.S. enters WWI	1913	California law prohibits all aliens who are ineligible for citizenship from owning land. Only "white persons" are eligible for naturalization. Leasing of land limited to three years. Similar laws eventually adopted in Washington, Oregon, Idaho, Montana, Arizona, New Mexico, Texas, Kansas, Louisiana, Missouri and Minnesota.	1919	Fred Korematsu is born in Oakland, CA.
1922	*Ozawa v. U.S.* — U.S. Supreme Court rules that naturalization is limited to "white persons and aliens of African nativity," thus legalizing previous practice of excluding Asians from citizenship.	1922	*Ozawa v. U.S.* — U.S. Supreme Court rules that naturalization is limited to "white persons and aliens of African nativity". Congress passes Cable Act, which provides that any woman marrying an alien ineligible for citizenship shall cease to be an American citizen. In practice, this means that anyone marrying an Issei would automatically lose citizenship. In marriages terminated by death or divorce, a Caucasian woman could regain citizenship, whereas a Nisei woman could not. Act is amended in 1931.	1923	Beulah Ong Kwoh is born in Stockton, CA.
				1924	Faustino "Peping" Baclig is born in Cabugao, Ilocos Sur, Philippines.
1929-33	Great Depression Era: 13 million people become unemployed in the U.S.	1924	Congress passes the Immigration Exclusion Act, ending all Asian immigration to the U.S., except for Filipinos who are subjects of the U.S.	1926	Philip Vera Cruz comes to the U.S.
1934	The Tydings-McDuffie Act declares the Philippines a commonwealth, guarantees independence in ten years.	1934	A section of the Tydings-McDuffie Act declares all Philippine-born Filipinos "aliens," and restricts their immigration to 50 Filipinos a year, separating many families.		
1939	Britain and France declare war on Germany, signaling the beginning of World War II.				
1940	President Roosevelt places embargo on most essential raw materials to Japan.				
1941	(December 7) — Japan bombs U.S. fleet and military base at Pearl Harbor. (December 8) — U.S. Congress declares war on Japan. (December 11) — U.S. declares war on Germany and Italy. Surrender of Bataan.	1941	(July 26) — President Franklin D. Roosevelt signs Military Order No. 81 "constituting a command designated as the United States Armed Forces of the Far East, which include the Philippine Department. Forces of the Commonwealth of the Philippines are called into service of the Armed Forces of the U.S. "for the period of the existing emergency and such other forces as may be designated to it."	1941	Young Filipinos are called to fight under the command of the U.S. military.

TIMELINE

Year	National/International Events	Year	Ethnic America Events	Year	"Untold Civil Rights" Events
1942	(June 4) — Battle of Midway cripples Japanese navy, a turning point in the war in the Pacific.	1942	(February 19) — President Franklin D. Roosevelt signs Executive Order 9066, forcing over 110,000 Japanese American citizens (Nisei) and immigrant parents (Issei) into internment camps during WWII solely based upon their ancestry. Today, the day is commemorated in Japanese American communities as a "Day of Remembrance".	1942	(April 9) — Bataan surrenders — 60,000 Filipino and 15,000 American soldiers are forced on the infamous Bataan Death March.
1943	(January 28) — U.S. War Department announces plans to organize all-Japanese American combat unit. As a result of a wartime alliance with China, the U.S. Congress repeals the Chinese Exclusion Act of 1882. The immigration quota for Chinese will remain low until the passage of the 1965 Immigration Act.	1943	(June 21) — *Hirabayashi v. U.S.* and *Yasui v. U.S.*: The U.S. Supreme Court rules that a curfew may be imposed against one group of American citizens based solely on ancestry and that Congress, in enacting Public Law 77-503, authorized the implementation of E.O. 9066 and provides criminal penalties for violation of orders of the military commander.		
1945	(August 6) — U.S. drops first atomic bomb on Hiroshima. (August 9) — Second atomic bomb drops on Nagasaki. (September 2) — Japan formally surrenders.	1944	(December 18) — *Korematsu v. U.S.*: The U.S. Supreme Court rules that one group of citizens may be singled out and expelled from their homes and imprisoned for several years without trial, based solely on their ancestry. (December 18) — In *ex parte Endo*, U.S. Supreme Court rules that War Relocation Authority (WRA) has no authority to detain a "concededly loyal" American citizen.	1944	*Korematsu v. U.S.* is heard by U.S. Supreme Court.
1946	President Harry S. Truman signs the Filipino Naturalization Acts allowing Filipinos to become citizens. The Philippines gains full independence.	1946	Congress passes and President Truman signs the Rescission Act of 1946, which denies Filipino soldiers who fought under the U.S. Armed Forces of the Far East the same rights given to other WWII veterans.	1946	Filipino soldiers are denied veterans rights despite fighting under the U.S. command.
				1948	The "Asparagus Strike", the first major agricultural strike after WWII, is led by unionized Filipino farm workers.
1950-53	Korean War			1950	K.W. Lee arrives in the U.S.
1952	Asian immigrants gain right to become citizens with the passage of the McCarran-Walter Immigration and Naturalization Act.	1952	(April 17) — California Supreme Court declares "alien land laws" in violation of the 14th Amendment by being racially discriminatory (*Fujii v. California*). (June 11) — McCarran-Walter Immigration and Naturalization Act is passed by Congress. Although restrictive, this law allows Japanese and other Asian immigrants to become naturalized citizens for the first time.		
1954	*Brown v. Board of Education* ends racial segregation in school.			1955	Vincent Chin is born in China and is later adopted by Lily and Bing Hing from a Chinese orphanage in 1961.
1959	Alaska becomes 49th state and Hawaii becomes 50th state.	1959	Hawaii becomes a state. Daniel Inouye is the first Japanese American elected to the U.S. House of Representatives. The Agricultural Workers Organizing Committee (AWOC) is established. Filipino Americans comprise majority of membership.		

TIMELINE

National/International Events	Ethnic America Events	"Untold Civil Rights" Events
1960-65 Civil Rights Movement **1960-75** Vietnam War	**1960** (February 1) — The sit-in movement begins in Greensboro, North Carolina; the goal is to desegregate public accommodation facilities throughout the South.	
1965 U.S. Congress passes the Immigration and Nationality Act, which abolishes "national origins" as basis for immigration and allows more immigration from Asia. Ferdinand E. Marcos becomes president of the Philippines	**1965** Agricultural Workers Organizing Committee (AWOC) begins strike against grape growers in Delano. The National Farm Workers Association (NFWA), primarily made up of Mexican Americans, joins the AWOC. The Delano grape strike will last five years and receives national attention. **1966** The NFWA and AWOC merge, forming the United Farm Workers (UFW), which becomes an affiliate of the American Federation of Labor and Congress of Industrial Organizations (AFL-CIO). Cesar Chavez leads march in CA, from Delano to Sacramento, focusing national attention on the plight of farm workers. **1968** (April 4) — Martin Luther King, Jr. is assassinated. His *Poor People's Campaign* proceeds but fails to achieve its goals.	**1965** Filipino farm workers begin strike against Delano, CA grape growers. East West Players is established — an Asian American theater organization that produces outstanding works and educational programs that give voice to the Asian Pacific American experience. **1969** UCLA Asian American Studies Center is established.
1972 Martial Law is declared in the Philippines under Ferdinand Marcos; in effect until 1986.	**1974** *Lau v. Nichols*: U.S. Supreme Court ruled that schools should provide students instruction in their native language. This ruling gave bilingual-bicultural education in the U.S. a tremendous boost. **1976** Two Mexican Americans, Jerry Apodaca and Raul Castro, are elected governors of New Mexico and Arizona respectively; first Hispanic governors since the early years of New Mexico statehood.	**1973** UFW begins construction of Agbayani Village for aging Filipino farm workers. **1974** Beulah Quo (Kwoh) wins an Emmy for the documentary *James Wong Howe: The Man and His Movies*.
1978 Congress passes a joint Congressional Resolution to commemorate Asian American Heritage Week during the first week of May. Congress will later vote to extend it to a month-long celebration.	**1977** The televised version of Alex Haley's *Roots* is viewed by more Americans (130 million) than any other television show in history. **1978** In the case of *Regents of the University of California v. Bakke*, the U.S. Supreme Court upholds the idea of affirmative action, but rules against strict racial quotas.	**1977** Philip Vera Cruz resigns from the United Farm Workers because of Cesar Chavez's support of Ferdinand Marcos.
1980 President Jimmy Carter signs bill to create the Commission on Wartime Relocation and Internment of Civilians (CWRIC) to review Executive Order 9066 and to recommend appropriate remedies.	**1982** *Plyler v. Do*: The U.S. Supreme Court reviews a Texas statute that withheld funds for the education of children who were not "legally admitted" into the U.S.; the Court strikes down the statute as a violation of the Equal Protection Clause of the Fourteenth Amendment. **1983** Fred Korematsu returns to the court. In response to a petition for a *writ of error coram nobis* by Korematsu, the federal district court vacates his conviction and rules that the government had no justification in issuing the internment orders. **1984** The Federal District Court in Portland, OR invalidates Minoru Yasui's 1942 conviction of violating a government curfew and "evacuation" orders.	**1982** Vincent Chin is killed in a Detroit, MI hate crime by two men with a baseball bat. Chol Soo Lee, a Korean American immigrant, is acquitted by jury in San Francisco, CA. Lee had spent nine years in prison for a killing he did not commit. His case aroused great community support. **1983** Vincent Chin's killers are given probation, sparking outrage in Asian American communities and a cry for justice. A federal grand jury later indicts the two killers on federal civil rights charges.

TIMELINE

National/International Events	Ethnic America Events	"Untold Civil Rights" Events
		1983 Asian Pacific American Legal Center (APALC) is co-founded by Stewart Kwoh.
		1985 Dr. Haing S. Ngor wins an Oscar for "Best Supporting Actor" at the Academy Awards for his first acting role in *The Killing Fields*. He became the first Asian American ever to receive an Oscar for acting.
	1986 The Federal District Court in Seattle, WA invalidates Gordon Hirabayashi's 1942 conviction for rejecting government curfew and "evacuation" orders. President Ronald Reagan signs Immigration Reform Control Act. Effort to discourage illegal immigration but Act also provides a pathway for legalization for some who had been continuously in the U.S. since January 1, 1982.	**1986** Manong Peping arrives in America with his family.
	1988 President Reagan signs the Civil Liberties Act of 1988. The law requires payment of $20,000 to each of the estimated 60,000 survivors of the Japanese internment during World War II. It includes an apology for the wrongdoing by the U.S. government.	**1987** Ronald Ebens, after a retrial in Cincinnati, OH, is acquitted of the murder of Vincent Chin. Ebens does not spend a single day in jail for the 1982 murder of Vincent Chin.
1989 Tragedy at Tiananmen results in tense Sino-American relations and U.S. trade sanctions.	**1989** Lawrence Douglas Wilder is elected governor of the state of Virginia, first African American to be elected a governor of a U.S. state.	
1990-91 Gulf War — U.S. declares war on Iraq.	**1990** Congress passes the Immigration Act of 1990, granting U.S. citizenship and limited veteran benefits to certain Filipino veterans who fought for the U.S. during WWII. 25,000 Filipino veterans were naturalized as U.S. citizens.	**1992** More than 2,500 Korean businesses are looted and burned as a result of riots in Los Angeles due to outrage over the Rodney King verdict.
	1992 Los Angeles Civil Unrest	**1994** Philip Vera Cruz dies in his hometown of Bakersfield, CA at the age of 89.
	1997 Filipino veterans demonstrate in Washington, D.C., and Los Angeles demanding equality and justice.	**1995** Raid on El Monte, CA sweatshop uncovers enslaved Thai garment workers.
1999 Taiwan-born U.S. citizen Wen Ho Lee, who worked at the Los Alamos Nuclear Laboratories, is arrested and imprisoned on false allegations of giving U.S. nuclear secrets to China; the original charges are later dropped and the judge in the case apologizes to Lee.	**1999** Wen Ho Lee case becomes a rallying point for Asian Americans who seek justice for unfair accusations of spying for China. The experiences of the enslaved Thai Garment Workers and the passage of Assembly Bill 633 opens door for retailer and manufacturer liability for the wages and working conditions of workers hired by contractors and sub-contactors. Gen. Eric K. Shinseki becomes the U.S. Army's 34th Chief of Staff. Shinseki is the only Japanese American and Asian American to be promoted to the U.S. Army's highest position and is the first four-star general of Asian descent in the U.S. military.	**1999** As a result of the El Monte raid, Assembly Bill 633, the toughest sweatshop legislation in the nation, is passed in CA. Joseph Ileto is gunned down by white supremacist — Buford Furrow.
2001 (September 11) — "9/11" Attacks on World Trade Center and U.S. Pentagon. President George W. Bush declares "War on Terror". U.S. and Britain targets Afghanistan in search for Osama bin Laden.		

TIMELINE

National/International Events	Ethnic America Events	"Untold Civil Rights" Events
	2000 — Twenty-two Asian American veterans were finally recognized for heroism and are awarded the nation's highest military award — the Medal of Honor. Many were Japanese Americans who volunteered for service from internments camps where their families had been relocated during WWII.	**2002** — (June 9) — Lily Chin dies at age 82 in Farmington Hills, MI. (October 23) — Beulah Quo (Kwoh) dies at age 79 in La Mesa, CA.
	2001 — Elaine Chao is appointed as Secretary of Labor; she is the first Chinese American and the first Asian American woman to be appointed to a President's cabinet in U.S. history.	**2004** — Amric Singh Rathour successfully challenges his dismissal over New York Police Department (NYPD) uniform policy and becomes an NYPD traffic officer.
2003 — U.S. invades Iraq.	**2003** — A new law (PL 108-170) is signed by President George Bush; it provides for official recognition and Veterans Administration (VA) medical care for approximately 11,000 living WWII Filipino veterans.	**2005** — (March 30) — Fred Korematsu dies at age 86 in Larkspur, CA.
2005 — Hurricane Katrina devastates Louisiana and Mississippi.	**2008** — U.S. Senate passes S.315 to award pension benefits to WWII Filipino veterans who fought under U.S. command. However, the House of Representatives fail to pass the bill and the bill is now officially dead. Barack Obama's election to be the nation's 44th president marks a milestone in U.S. history.	**2008** — (August 14) — Former Thai slave laborers become U.S. citizens.
2006 — Lt. Ehren Watada, contending that the War in Iraq is illegal, becomes the first commissioned officer to refuse orders to deploy to Iraq. His first court-martial in 2007 ends in a mistrial. On May 6, 2009, the 9th U.S. Circuit Court of Appeals drops the government's case against him.	**2009** — President Obama includes in his Cabinet: Attorney General Eric Holder (Justice) — first African American to hold this position; Secretary Steven Chu (Energy) — first Asian American to hold this position; Gary Locke (Commerce) — first Chinese American to hold this position; Secretary Hilda Solis (Labor) — first Hispanic woman to serve as a secretary in Cabinet; Secretary Eric Shinseki (Veterans Affairs) — first Asian American to hold this position.	**2009** — As part of HR 1, the American Recovery and Reinvestment Act of 2009, Filipino veterans finally succeed in gaining recognition for their military service as U.S. veterans. Surviving veterans to receive one-time payments of $15,000 to Filipino American veterans residing in the U.S. or in the Philippines, and $9,000 to veterans who are Philippine citizens. It also contains a provision for spouses and protects eligibility for benefits currently received by veterans.
2008 — The U.S. suffers disastrous economic downturn in all major sectors. The economic crisis is felt worldwide. Barack Obama, Democratic Senator from IL, is elected to be the nation's 44th President; making him the first president of African American descent in the history of the U.S.	U.S. Congress passes HR 1, the American Recovery and Reinvestment Act of 2009 — the economic stimulus bill. The Act includes Filipino WWII veterans' legislation.	
2009 — Eric Holder is appointed as the nation's first African American attorney general. The U.S. Congress approves HR 1, the American Recovery and Reinvestment Act of 2009, the economic stimulus bill, which includes legislation regarding Filipino World War II veterans.		

Contributors

Editors

Stewart Kwoh is the president and executive director of the Asian Pacific American Legal Center of Southern California (APALC), the largest and most diverse legal assistance and civil rights organization targeting Asian Pacific Americans in the United States. He is the co-author of *Searching for the Uncommon Common Ground: New Dimensions on Race in America*, 2002. Kwoh was named a MacArthur Foundation Fellow in 1998. He is the first Asian American attorney and human rights activist to receive this highly prestigious recognition, often referred to as a "genius grant." He is on the board of the Committee of 100, a national organization of Chinese American leaders. He is also on the board of many community organizations and foundations, and has received many awards from diverse organizations. He has also been president of the Los Angeles City Human Relations Commission.

Russell C. Leong is the editor of UCLA's *Amerasia Journal*, the interdisciplinary journal of Asian American Studies. He is an adjunct professor of English and Asian American Studies, and also serves as the project head of the U.S./China Media Brief at UCLA. *www.uschina-mediabrief.com*

Authors

May Lee Heye is a trial attorney for the United States Department of Justice Antitrust Division, where she prosecutes white collar crime. Prior to joining the Department of Justice, she worked in private practice. She has volunteered for the Asian Law Caucus.

Bill Ong Hing is a professor of Law at the University of California, Davis, where he teaches Judicial Process, Negotiations, Public Service Strategies, Asian American History, and directs the law school clinical program. In addition to these duties, Professor Hing is the author of numerous academic and practice-oriented books, and articles on immigration policy and race relations. Among his other achievements, he is also the founder of, and continues to volunteer as General Counsel for, the Immigrant Legal Resource Center in San Francisco.

Dale Minami is an attorney and partner with Minami Tamaki LLP in San Francisco, specializing in personal injury and entertainment law. He has been involved in significant litigation involving the civil rights of Asian Pacific Americans and other minorities, including: *Korematsu v. United States*, *United Pilipinos for Affirmative Action v. California Blue Shield*, *Spokane JACL v. Washington State University*, and other landmark cases. He was a co-founder of the Asian Law Caucus, Inc., a community-interest law firm, a co-founder of the Asian American Bar Association of the Greater Bay Area, the first Asian American Bar Association in the United States, the Asian Pacific Bar of California and the Coalition of Asian Pacific Americans, a registered political action committee.

Karen Narasaki is the president and executive director of the Asian American Justice Center, formerly known as the National Asian Pacific American Legal Consortium. The AAJC is a national nonprofit, nonpartisan organization that works to advance the human and civil rights of Asian Americans through advocacy, public policy, public education, and litigation.

Angela Oh is an attorney, teacher, and public lecturer. Her law firm, Oh & Barrera, LLP, is based in Los Angeles. The firm offers representation in state and federal criminal matters and civil rights. The various commissions and boards she has served include the California Commission on Access to Justice and the board of directors for Lawyers Mutual Insurance Co., and the Washington, D.C.-based Women's Policy, Inc. and the Western Justice Center Foundation.

Mary Ellen Kwoh Shu is blessed to come from a family of many heroes — her mother, Beulah Quo, her father, Edwin, and her brother, Stewart. She and her husband, Jack, have three children — Christina, Teddy, and Julia — and have made their home in La Mesa, California. A former psychiatric social worker, Mary Ellen is now enjoying another career as an elementary school librarian.

Julie Su is Litigation Director at the Asian Pacific American Legal Center of Southern California (APALC). She is also a MacArthur Fellow, recipient of the Reebok International Human Rights Awards, and was named one of the "Top 75 Women Litigators" in California by the *Daily Journal*. Su was the lead attorney for the Thai and Latino workers.

Casimiro Urbano Tolentino is a labor and civil rights lawyer. He has been an administrative law judge II for the state of California since 1992. He was assistant chief counsel for the Department of Fair Employment and Housing for six years enforcing California's civil rights laws, and was a regional attorney and regional director for the Agricultural Labor Relations Board. He has also co-founded numerous organizations including the Pilipino American Bar Association and the board of the Asian Pacific American Legal Consortium (a civil rights advocate for the Asian Pacific communities based in Washington, D.C.), now the Asian American Justice Center.

Kent Wong is director of the UCLA Center for Labor Research and Education, where he teaches Labor Studies and Asian American Studies. Kent has also served as national president of the Asian Pacific American Labor Alliance, and the United Association for Labor Education.

Eric Yamamoto is an internationally recognized law professor at the University of Hawai'i William S. Richardson School of Law. He is known for his legal work and scholarship on civil rights and racial justice, with an emphasis on reparations for historic injustice. He is a founding member of the Equal Justice Society and speaks regularly across the country and internationally on issues of racial reconciliation, reparations, civil and human rights and national security and civil liberties. In 1983 and 1984, Professor Yamamoto served as a member of Fred Korematsu's *coram nobis* legal team.

Helen Zia is the author of *Asian American Dreams: The Emergence of an American People* (Farrar, Straus and Giroux, 2001). She is board co-chair of the Women's Media Center and a member of the Committee of 100, a national organization of Chinese American leaders.

Curriculum Consultant

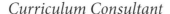

Esther R. Taira currently consults for organizations including the Los Angeles Unified School District, the Go for Broke Education Center, and the Asian Pacific American Legal Center of Southern California. She was the instructional specialist in charge of the Los Angeles Unified School District's Multicultural Unit until her retirement in 2002. In her 36 years with the district, she wrote a number of district curriculum guides and developed and presented workshops.

Editorial Assistants

Irene Lee is a fourth-year undergraduate majoring in Asian American Studies at UCLA. Inspired by her experiences both in school and at the APALC, she hopes to pursue a profession that is dedicated to improving conditions for minority and low-income communities. On and off campus, she has been involved with: the Rotary Interact Club, Unicamp, and the Asian Pacific American Legal Center.

Ryan Khamkongsay did his undergraduate studies at USC as an Economics major, while serving as a Sergeant in the U.S. Army National Guard. He currently works at the Asian Pacific American Legal Center in Program Administration. Outside of APALC, he is an advocate for the Thai/ Laotian American communities and an activist for marriage equality.

Jieun Jacobs attended UC Berkeley as an undergraduate, majoring in History while lettering on the women's tennis team. She is currently attending Southwestern Law School's two-year SCALE program and will graduate with a J.D. in May 2009. She has been a volunteer and law clerk at the Asian Pacific American Legal Center.

Organizations

The mission of the **Asian Pacific American Legal Center of Southern California (APALC)** is to advocate for civil rights, provide legal services and education, and build coalitions to positively influence and impact Asian Pacific Americans and to create a more equitable and harmonious society.

APALC was founded in 1983 with broad community based support and is now the largest organization in the country focused on meeting the legal needs of one of the nation's fastest growing populations. APALC serves more than 15,000 individuals and organizations each year through direct services, community education, training, and technical assistance.

APALC is a unique organization that merges the work of a traditional legal service provider and a civil rights organization. To achieve its goals of justice and equality, APALC draws on four strategies: direct legal services; impact litigation; policy analysis and advocacy; and leadership development.

As a direct legal services provider, APALC serves the diverse APA communities with intake, legal counseling, education, and representation in poverty law areas such as family law and domestic violence, consumer rights, immigration, and housing. Through its staff and volunteers, it has the capacity to facilitate numerous languages including Korean, Japanese, Mandarin, Cantonese, Khmer, Indonesian, and Vietnamese, along with English and Spanish. APALC is the only legal service provider in Los Angeles County that maintains this type of language capacity, and thus is an important resource for indigent monolingual or limited English speaking APAs who are in need of legal assistance.

At the same time, as a civil rights advocacy organization APALC has been involved with a wide range of civil rights issues, including hate crimes monitoring, police-community relations, voting rights, and immigrant rights. In addition, APALC takes a leadership role in promoting collaboration with other ethnic groups, advocacy groups, and social service providers on a range of issues concerning the Los Angeles community at large.

In its litigation strategy area, APALC, along with other advocates, led the groundbreaking workers' rights lawsuit, *Bureerong v. Uvawas*, and worked with Thai and Latino garment workers to hold manufacturers and retailers accountable for sweatshop conditions. APALC continues to use a grassroots model of litigation that includes casework, outreach, education, and policy advocacy, to empower garment workers to engage in a broader movement for social justice.

Finally, APALC's focus on interethnic relations and multiracial coalition building is evident in its youth, parent, and community-focused leadership development programs, as well as in its work in garment workers' rights, hate crimes prevention, and coalition building within the API community. In all of these areas, APALC is explicitly multi- and cross-racial in its approach and seeks to develop both youth and adult advocates and leaders whose work can cross-racial, ethnic, geographic, and other boundaries.

APALC is affiliated with the Asian American Justice Center.

For more information, please visit the official APALC website: *http://www.apalc.org* or call: 213-977-7500.

The **UCLA Asian American Studies Center (AASC)** is one of four ethnic studies centers at the University of California, Los Angeles. Established in 1969, the Center is recognized as the premier research, publications, and teaching program in the field of Asian American Studies. Together with the department of Asian American Studies, UCLA has the largest undergraduate and graduate program in Asian American Studies in the nation with faculty from all disciplines of the humanities and social sciences. Its renowned Press publishes the *Amerasia Journal* and *AAPI Nexus*.

Transforming Civil Society for the 21st Century

In 2009, the Center marked its 40th anniversary. It achieved this major milestone through the collective dedication of thousands of alumni, community leaders, donors, students, staff, and faculty.

"The Asian American Studies Center at UCLA is indisputably the leading Asian American Studies center in the country and an exemplary ethnic studies center of any kind, the gold standard against which all the rest are measured . . . While enjoying widespread community support, particularly in the vast Southern California region, it serves the entire nation through its research and policy work, its publications, library and archives," according to a recent external review of national experts in the field of Asian American Studies.

The UCLA Asian American Studies Center continues to pursue and produce collaborative research, publications, archives, and public programming to educate and to serve the public and to transform civil society for the 21st Century.

— Don T. Nakanishi, Director

PROGRAMS

Research

Curriculum Development

UCLA Asian American Studies Press

Library and Archives

Leadership Training

New Media and Technology

EthnoCommunications

U.S./China Media and Communications Program

Community Partners

Public Programming

Director: Don T. Nakanishi

For more information: *http://www.aasc.ucla.edu/* or call: 310-825-2974.

Acknowledgments

Patricia Buske, Carmina Ocampo, Rebecca Shea, Karin Wang, Bernice Yau, Clayton Yeung
Kavita Aggarwal, Alice Kim, Stephanie Snipes, Jennifer H. Wang

Russell C. Leong, Mary Uyematsu Kao, Stephanie D. Santos, Ying M. Tu

Don T. Nakanishi, Robert A. Nakamura, Melany dela Cruz-Viesca, Russell C. Leong, Stephanie D. Santos,
Mary Uyematsu Kao, Betty Leung, Tam Nguyen, Ann Chau, Ying M. Tu, Marjorie Lee, Meg Malpaya Thornton,
Gena Hamamoto

We deeply appreciate the contribution of the Beulah Kwoh Fellowship Fund
for the printing of this book.

Notes